The Scientific Credibility
of Folk Psychology

The Scientific Credibility
of Folk Psychology

Garth Fletcher
University of Canterbury

RECEIVED

AUG 26 1996

CMC ALPINE CAMPUS
LEARNING RESOURCE CENTER

LEA LAWRENCE ERLBAUM ASSOCIATES, PUBLISHERS
1995   Mahwah, New Jersey

Lawrence Erlbaum Associates, Inc., Publishers
10 Industrial Avenue
Mahwah, New Jersey 07430

Library of Congress Cataloging-in-Publication Data

Fletcher, Garth J. O.
The scientific credibility of folk psychology / Garth
Fletcher.
p. cm.
Includes bibliographical references and index.
ISBN 0-8058-1570-8 (alk paper). -- ISBN 0-8058-
1571-6 (pbk. : alk. paper)
1. Psychology--Philosophy. 2. Ethnopsychology. 3.
Cognitive science. I. Title.
BF38.F58 1995
150'.1--dc20   95-24235
                                                    CIP

Books published by Lawrence Erlbaum Associates are printed
on acid-free paper, and their bindings are chosen for strength
and durability.

Printed in the United States of America
10 9 8 7 6 5 4 3 2 1

For my parents, *Alan* and *Joan Fletcher*

Contents

Preface

The examination and evaluation of folk psychology and lay cognition has been predominantly carried out in two domains: personality and social psychology (especially social cognition), and the philosophy of psychology. Yet, work in these two areas has largely proceeded independently. The psychological literature is mainly empirical and not given to the kind of overarching analysis attempted in this book (with some important exceptions, to be sure). The philosophical literature, in turn, has mostly ignored the work carried out in social psychology—an odd fact, given the increasingly naturalistic orientation adopted by philosophers working in the cognitive science field. The assumption on which this volume is founded is that a proper comparison between scientific cognition and folk ways of thought rests on an adequate analysis of both science and folk psychology. In this book I have attempted both this task and an analysis of the intricate, and often hidden, links between the two spheres. Thus, this book represents an integration of material from social psychology, cognitive science, and the philosophy of science.

I am only too aware of the ambitious nature of this project, and that such interdisciplinary attempts in the past have often ended up satisfying neither psychologists nor philosophers. Whether I have fared any better I leave to the reader to decide. However, I have striven to write a concise and readable treatise that will be intelligible to, and of interest for, both psychologists and philosophers.

ACKNOWLEDGMENTS

Many people are to thank for this book. I thank Leslie Zebrowitz and the faculty at Brandeis University for providing an encouraging and supportive environment during 1992, when I was on sabbatical at that institution and wrote the first half of this book. Simon Kemp and Jacqui Duxbury manfully read and provided superb critical notes on the entire manuscript. Numerous others provided feedback on individual chapters, or on working papers on which some of the chapters were built, including Tony Atkinson, Jack Copland, Alan Fletcher, John Fletcher, John Greenwood, Brian Haig, Craig Lange, Glenn Reeder, Gill Rhodes, Barrie Stacey, Geoff Thomas, Tanya Tremewan, and Tony Ward. I especially thank Brian Haig for his unstinting help over the years, and Simon Kemp for his willingness to engage in many hours of lively debate (often accompanied by the imbibing of red wine), and his remarkable ability to ask the right critical questions no matter how inebriated.

—*Garth Fletcher*

Chapter 1
Folk Psychology: Crock or Touchstone?

This book deals with the relations between psychology and common sense—a complex and subtle topic that has been a hotbed of debate within both psychology and philosophy for many years. In this introduction I lay the groundwork for the book by first running briefly over the history of the topic in both philosophy and psychology. Next, some of the key questions and issues dealt with are sketched out, with a description of the book's orientation and goals.

Attitudes in both philosophy and psychology toward folk psychology have ranged from the reverential to the dismissive. In the 1950s and 1960s, under the influence of Wittgenstein and the ordinary language school, philosophers often adopted eulogistic approaches to common sense. For example, Peters (1960), in his book _The Concept of Motivation_, argued that

> the difficulty about developing a science of psychology is that, in a sense, we already know too much about human behavior, albeit in a rather uncoordinated manner. Common-sense, which is incorporated in the concepts of ordinary language, has creamed off most of the vital distinctions. Psychology has the task of sytematizing what is already known and adding bits of special theory to supplement common-sense. (p. 155)

As Yang inevitably follows Ying, a new breed of philosopher in the last two decades has argued that folk psychology is a crock, doomed to be replaced by psychological theories with sterner scientific credentials—a position known as _eliminative materialism_. This group of philosophers, led by Paul Churchland, are members of a growing and influential brand of philosophy that is naturalistic and scientific in orientation, and that pays special attention to psychological research concerned with the mind or the brain. Indeed, the burgeoning field of cognitive science as a discipline includes the philosophy of the mind as one of its defining

1

assortment of subdisciplines along with cognitive psychology, engineering, neuropsychology, and artificial intelligence.

The relation between folk psychology and scientific psychology has become an important topic in cognitive science, spawning several anthologies and a host of articles in philosophical journals. The thesis of eliminative materialism, in particular, has come under considerable attack, with more than one philosopher springing to the defense of folk psychology. In due course, I discuss what I take to be some of the key arguments advanced in this arena (especially in chapter 7). In so doing, I argue that the discussion in the philosophical literature has assumed an unduly simplistic notion of what folk psychology amounts to, and that much can be learned from consulting the relevant research in social psychology or social cognition.

It turns out, for example, that the most rigorous empirical analysis of the rationality or scientific credibility of folk cognition, combined with a good dose of theoretical argument, has taken place in social psychology, not cognitive psychology. However, philosophers working within the cognitive science tradition have, by and large, not consulted this extensive literature. In contrast, in this book I extensively review both the empirical research and associated theoretical disputes from social psychology in addressing the relation between folk psychology and scientific psychology.

Not that social psychologists, or, indeed, any other kind of psychologist, speak with one voice in assessing the scientific value of folk psychology. As in philosophical circles, the popular attitudes toward common sense in psychology have gone through cycles, with dissenting voices, of course, always present.

Radical behaviorism, for example, is famously derogatory about common sense. Its most noted proponent, Skinner (1974), wrote:

> The disastrous results of common sense in the management of behavior are evident in every walk of life, from international affairs to the care of a baby, and we shall continue to be inept in these fields, until a scientific analysis clarifies the advantage of a more effective technology. It will then be obvious that the results are due to more than common sense. (p. 234)

However, it is not merely that Skinner preferred science to common sense. Rather he viewed folk psychology as the central impediment to the development of science and human progress. Thus, Skinner (1978) wrote that the main obstacle to the utilization of behavioral science is "the entrenchment of old practices—in this case the old ways of thinking about human behavior. Antiquated theories ingrained in our language and our culture stand in the way of promising scientific alternatives" (p. 85).

The history of social psychology also reveals attitudes and views that range from the reverential to the dismissive. One of the founders of modern social psychology, Heider, attempted to develop an understanding of lay psychology by careful conceptual analysis of the theoretical structures underlying everyday language. Heider (1958) argued that the analysis of these conceptual structures could play an important role in describing lay cognitive processes, and in developing a theory to explain such processes. In short, Heider took folk psychology seriously. In his words, "the ordinary person has a great and profound understanding of himself [sic] and other people which, though unformulated or only vaguely conceived, enables him [sic] to interact with others in more or less adaptive ways" (p. 2).

In contrast, textbooks in social psychology commonly seek to distance the discipline from folk psychology. This is almost invariably accomplished by pointing out that commonsense maxims abound that are contradictory (e.g., "birds of a feather flock together" vs. "opposites attract"), and perhaps also mentioning the odd social inference bias that lay social cognition is cursed with (e.g., hindsight bias, overconfidence in social judgments, ignoring base rates). The proposed replacement for folk psychology (surprise! surprise!) is held to be a (social) psychological science that is grounded in research and data.

In general, doubts about the validity or rationality of lay social cognition reached their peak in personality and social psychology in the 1980s. Personality psychology was in the throes of a debate concerning whether behavior was consistent across situations, and, although the jury was still out on the issue, powerful voices and persuasive data suggested that the concept of personality traits was a shibboleth of folk psychology. As Nisbett and Ross (1980) said, "the personality theorists' (and the layperson's) conviction that there are strong cross-situational consistencies in behavior may be seen as merely another instance of theory-driven covariation assessments operating in the face of contrary evidence" (p. 112).

In social cognition circles, a flood of research on errors and biases apparently demonstrated that laypeople were subject to an extraordinary range of invidious social judgment biases. Laypeople were purported to underestimate the causal role of situational determinants of behavior and overestimate the role of personal determinants (the so-called fundamental attribution error), to be poor statisticians, to be unduly influenced by prior theories while underutilizing data, and much more. As Fiske and Taylor (1984) concluded in their textbook, *Social Cognition,* in describing the lay psychologist, "Instead of a naive scientist entering the environment in search of the truth, we find the rather unflattering picture of a charlatan trying to make the data come out in a manner most advantageous to his or her already held theories" (p. 88).

Just as in philosophy, this rather bleak view of human rationality has been increasingly challenged over the last decade, with the consensus swinging back toward the more respectful stance adopted by Heider. This body of research and theorizing is summarized and discussed in chapters 6 and 7.

As can be seen, then, there is considerable dispute both within philosophy and psychology concerning the evaluation of folk psychology. The analysis offered in this book is based around several claims or strategies.

First, I have attempted to bring the tools and evidence from both philosophy and (social) psychology to the issues at hand. This task was approached with some trepidation, as, in my experience, this sort of interdisciplinary effort typically satisfies neither philosophers nor psychologists. I leave it to the reader to decide how successful I have been.

Second, one of my basic contentions is that a lacuna in cognitive science, philosophy, and psychology that has had dire consequences is that insufficient attention has been given to answering two critical empirical questions: First, what is the nature of folk psychology? and, second, what is the nature of the overlap between folk psychology and scientific psychology?

There is certainly a consensus that folk psychology represents something that is shared and used by us all in everyday life. Beyond, these two points, however, there is considerable divergence of opinion, and understanding the nature of folk psychology and its relation to psychology assume considerable complexity. Chapters 2, 3, and 4 are devoted to answering these two questions, although I periodically return to them throughout the book, particularly in chapters 6 and 7, where I turn to the prescriptive question of what the relationship should be between folk psychology and scientific psychology.

Another gap that I think exists in both the philosophical and psychological literature in this domain is the need for an explicit normative account of scientific inference. If judgments about the rationality or scientific probity of lay psychological theory or particular social judgments are advanced (and they regularly are), then some normative standard is being wittingly or unwittingly applied. Indeed, one of my complaints with the considerable body of research in social cognition dealing with biases and errors in social inference, is that I believe the normative (and supposedly scientific) standards used are often suspect. Accordingly, in chapter 5, I have set up an explicit model of scientific inference borrowed largely from sources in the philosophy of science. I then use this model as an organizing framework for the subsequent analysis and review of the empirical and theoretical work in relation to the scientific credibility of folk psychology in chapters 5, 6, and 7.

If this outline seems ambitious for one slim(ish) volume, it is. However, I do not pretend to offer a systematic review of all the issues and arguments involved (although I have provided references for those who wish to read further). Instead, my approach is to pluck out and express what I understand to be the kernels of the arguments. For those readers who wish to consult an even more expurgated version of this book, I have summarized the main arguments and issues raised in the concluding chapter.

Chapter 2
The Nature of Folk Psychology

In any analysis of the links between scientific psychology and folk psychology, the proposed nature and definition of folk psychology will be pivotal. Indeed, I argue later that some of the most cited and trenchant arguments directed against the viability of folk psychology by philosophers rest on a somewhat restrictive and superficial account of the beast in question. The analysis of folk psychology in this chapter is unavoidably general, as this concept turns out to be a slippery customer indeed. The aim is to erect sufficient conceptual scaffolding from which to build the remainder of my analysis and arguments.

As a beginning point, *folk psychology* might be defined as a cultural group's body of shared beliefs or ways of thinking about the world. The notion that folk psychology is shared is an important ingredient in this definition—I return at various times to this aspect. A second feature of this definition is that folk psychology refers either to the content of thought or beliefs, or to underlying process or structure. This distinction between content and process is actually present in everyday usage of the term. People often say that certain beliefs are just "common sense"; that is, they are part of our commonsense store of knowledge. Conversely, the term is sometimes used to refer to the shared canons and rules that define the reasonable or correct way of thinking; for example we sometimes urge people to use their common sense (think properly or clearly) in making decisions or judgments.

So, folk psychology potentially covers everything that psychologists are interested in—in broad terms, the explanation, prediction, and control of human behavior and experience. Even though this represents an enormous field, it nevertheless excludes a good deal of commonsense thought. For example, it rules out everyday theories concerning the movement and behavior of inanimate objects (a naive physics) and commonsense biological theories. Some psychologists are, of course, interested in the development and nature of lay physical and biological theories, but my point here is that such lay theories are not themselves psychological theories. The domain of interest, for the purposes of this book, concerns those lay theories that are psychological in nature.

In addition, many areas of interest to psychologists may be relatively untouched by folk psychology including neuropsychology, our perceptual systems including the visual and auditory systems, language learning, and so forth. In contrast, folk psychology does appear to have a lot to say in relation to social psychology, personality, and, to a lesser extent, cognitive psychology. Accordingly, it is these three latter areas of psychology that I focus on throughout the book.

In the first section of this chapter I distinguish three aspects in the content of folk psychology: proverbs and fables, general shared beliefs and attitudes, and shared fundamental beliefs. Second, I deal with folk psychology in terms of shared underlying cognitive structures and processes. Third, the relations between the two levels (content and process) are analyzed, and the differences between folk psychology and idiosyncratic cognition or lay theory discussed.

THE CONTENT OF FOLK PSYCHOLOGY: THREE KINDS OF SHARED BELIEF

Proverbs and Fables

This class of items is often what springs to mind when the term *common sense* is used by laypeople or psychologists alike. Such beliefs are often expressed in proverbs, sometimes as valuable guides for behavior (e.g., "a stitch in time saves nine," "look before you leap"), and sometimes as causal generalizations or psychological principles (e.g., "clothes maketh the man," "birds of a feather flock together"). They may also be expressed in a more long-winded fashion as allegories or fables.

The stock of proverbs and aphorisms in our culture is vast. According to the list complied by Erasmus (1508), there are more than 3,000 proverbs to be garnered from antiquarian sources, and of course there are thousands more witty or helpful epithets that derive from modern literary sources. This stock of epithets is also constantly being added to from popular culture, some being derived from modern technology that would be unintelligible to earlier generations (e.g., "garbage in, garbage out").

Moreover, it is common for groups and institutions within society to develop their own purpose-built set of slogans or proverbs, some of which may be idiosyncratic. Such institutions would include religious organizations, businesses, schools, social clubs, sports teams, and therapeutic communities. For example, Bassin (1983) remarked on the prevalence and use of slogans and proverbs in drug treatment programs, and noted that they are typically displayed prominently and sometimes recited as a group mantra. Some examples: "There is no free lunch"; "Think, think, think"; "The door swings both ways"; "What goes around comes around"; "No pain without gain"; "When the going gets tough, the tough get going"; "Pride comes before a fall"; and "Don't drink even if your ass is on fire." No prizes for guessing that the last proverb is from Alcoholics Anonymous!

Now proverbs undoubtedly serve a number of psychological and sociological functions including the building and reinforcement of a social ideology, a means of regulating behavior, and the building of social cohesion. Moreover, even a casual perusal of any set of proverbs or slogans will reveal a strong moral or evaluative component. In Aesop's fables and associated proverbs, for example, lust, greed, hubris, ambition, conceit, and stupidity (often accompanied by self-deception) often lead to one's downfall. In contrast, moderation, loyalty, prudence, and sober self-knowledge are usually rewarded. However, it would be a mistake to classify such proverbs simply in moral or evaluative terms, for they also contain a set of causal generalizations or psychological insights that can be evaluated in terms of their truth value or scientific usefulness.

Not surprisingly, given the apparent banality of many proverbs, it is easy to lampoon the validity or usefulness of this body of maxims. It is common, for example, for introductory chapters in social psychology textbooks to distance the discipline of social psychology from common sense by juxtaposing contradictory proverbs, such as "many hands make light work" and "too many cooks spoil the broth." What folk psychology cannot tell us, so goes the standard textbook spiel, are the conditions under which each generalization is true. For that we need psychological research.

A demonstration of the apparent vacuity of folk psychology was provided by Tiegen (1986), who asked students to rate the truth value of actual proverbs and their opposites. He found that both actual and reversed proverbs were given similar truth ratings, with reversed proverbs often being thought truer than the actual proverbs; for example, the reversed false proverb "love is stronger than fear" was rated as truer than the original "fear is stronger than love."

In defense of this body of commonsense formulations, it could be pointed out that proverbs and the like are, after all, one-liners. By their very nature they need to be used judiciously, with the understanding that they apply better in some contexts than others (see Furnham, 1988). Indeed, there exists a proverb that indicates the danger in willy-nilly use of such maxims: "Wise men make proverbs and fools repeat them." There are obvious inherent limitations in any aphorism or pithy piece of psychological wisdom. Any program of research or theory in psychology, no matter how sophisticated, would tend to sound naively simplistic and too sweeping to be taken seriously as a "scientific" formulation when reduced to a one-line conclusion (or sound suspiciously similar to some commonsense maxim).

Interestingly, one of the criticisms one often hears from students in their first encounters with social psychology is that it is essentially common sense, that they knew it all along. This charge of obviousness is usually repelled by textbook authors by explaining such judgments represent the "hindsight" bias (Fischhoff & Beyth, 1975)—the tendency to retrospectively inflate one's confidence in knowing or believing something after one has obtained confirmatory evidence. Ironically, such a defense can equally well be applied to the banality that attaches to commonsense formulations, although I have never seen it defended this way. Indeed, knowledge of such a bias appears to be widespread. For example, I have noticed that in media interviews, when asked retrospectively to assess their prior judgments of a sporting event (e.g., "Did you think you would win?"), people will commonly preface their answers with such caveats as "with 20/20 hindsight" or "it is easy to be wise after the event." As this example illustrates, the hindsight bias is itself represented in proverbs.

Proverbial warnings against the incipient tendency to obtain 20/20 hindsight reflects one further feature of our "conventional wisdom" that I believe is important; namely, a good deal of proverbial advice is actually directed at ordinary or commonplace ways of acting or thinking that are assumed to be in error or simply stupid. This central idea is clearly apparent, for example, in many fables. Consider, for example, the following Aesop's fables: The fox who judged the unobtainable grapes to be sour, the poor toad who blew apart when it imagined it could puff itself up to the size of a bull, and the ass who mistakenly attributed cowardice to the lion when he observed it being frightened by a crowing rooster and was subsequently eaten. I have deliberately chosen these fables because they illustrate three theories or judgmental biases much studied by social psychologists over the last few decades: Cognitive dissonance theory, overconfidence or overoptimism in one's personal powers, and the fundamental attribution error, respectively (see chapter 6).The role of such cautionary tales only make sense when such folk wisdom is set against an assumed backdrop of prevalent human foolishness or error-prone thinking.

This feature of fables and proverbs is critical because it suggests that there are individual differences in the ability of people to follow sensible rules or to fall prey to human folly. I return to this theme in chapter 6 when I discuss the psychological research that has postulated the widespread prevalence of biases and errors in human social cognition.

There are many examples of proverbs or fables that appear linked to psychological research or theories. Rogers (1990) tracked down 34 examples of proverbs for which there exist research that can be interpreted as tests of their validity (e.g., "birds of a feather flock together," "ignorance is bliss," "once bitten twice shy," and so forth). To what extent such psychological research was actually motivated by the accompanying proverbial wisdom is hard to say, but it seems likely that such an accessible knowledge base has had some role in the development of psychological research and theorizing.

To what extent psychologists should utilize such folk wisdom in their research is a major question I deal with at length later on. For now, I merely note that I can think of no reason or argument why psychologists should commit themselves a priori to the truth value of this component of folk psychology.

General Shared Beliefs and Attitudes

Proverbs and fables are but one subset of commonly shared beliefs in any community. There are in fact a huge number of beliefs that are widely shared and, hence, can be thought of as commonsensical, but that are not embedded in stories or expressed as proverbs: to cite just a few relevant to the psychological domain—poor communication causes relationship breakdown, politicians cannot be trusted, severe punishment deters criminals, hard work leads to success, men are more aggressive than women, Blacks are more violent than Whites, and homosexuality is wrong.

To begin with, it is clear that varying proportions of people in Western cultures would regard these beliefs as true. Indeed, it is possible, in Western society, to find sane individuals who do not hold to any given particular belief, no matter how bizarre such a denial might be—there are folk, for example, who deny evolution, or that the earth is round. Polls of Americans have also revealed an astonishing level of agreement with beliefs than one might thought were long since buried. For example, one Gallup poll reported that 57% of Americans believe in UFOs, 54% in angels, 51% in ESP, 39% in devils, 29% in astrology, and 10% in ghosts and witches.

Clearly, one cannot require a given belief to attain 100% allegiance in order to count as a commonsense belief. However, it is hard to say what level of consensus needs to be obtained in order for a particular belief to be regarded as part of folk psychology. It is certainly the case, for example, that homosexuality is widely regarded as deviant—polls conducted over a 9-year period in the United States (1973–1982) found that around 70% of respondents agreed that homosexuality was always wrong, whereas only 14% said that homosexuality was never wrong (Myers, 1993). This degree of unanimity is probably enough to confer and legitimate the sort of taken-for-granted, obvious quality that commonsense beliefs have.

In addition, such social, stereotypical beliefs and attitudes are labile in Western cultures. For example, attitudes connected with race and gender have become markedly more liberal over the last half century. In 1942, fewer than one third of all U.S. Whites supported school integration; in 1980, support for this issue stood at 90%. In 1937, just over 20% of Americans approved of married women working and 30% would have voted for a qualified woman as president; by 1986, both figures had soared to over 80% (see Myers, 1993).

It is probable that such changes in beliefs and attitudes are wrought, at least in part, through widespread debate of such beliefs in our educational institutions, the media, and governmental bodies, all fueled by the efforts of minority groups who have been discriminated against (women, Blacks, homosexuals, etc.). Beliefs that Blacks are inferior, that women are not fitted for public office, that homosexuals are sick or sinful or both, at certain times in our history were cultural truisms that were largely part of folk knowledge—neither defended not debated. Faced with arguments and opposing points of view, such beliefs are dragged, kicking and screaming, into the public arena where they need to be explicitly defended, for which arguments need to be provided, and for which the seeds of doubt may subsequently be sown. Interestingly, social psychologists have known for some time that tacitly held beliefs that appear self-evident or obvious (cultural truisms) are particularly susceptible to attack. For example, Ross, McFarland, and Fletcher (1981) were able to induce massive changes in the beliefs that people had concerning the value of toothbrushing and bathing, with relative ease, by exposing them to short bogus interviews with a supposed expert who argued that excessive bathing and molar brushing were harmful.

The same sort of conclusion drawn earlier concerning the role of proverbial wisdom vis-à-vis psychology is clearly applicable here; namely, that such a network of beliefs almost certainly influences psychological theorizing and research, but that it would appear to be remarkably silly for psychologists to commit themselves a priori to the truth (or falsity) of such beliefs.

Still, one could reasonably argue (and some psychologists and philosophers do) that there is a certain category of beliefs that are, practically speaking unanimous, that are seldom made explicit, but that nevertheless must be true: I now turn to a discussion of such fundamental beliefs.

Shared Fundamental Beliefs

The sort of beliefs I have in mind here are those bedrock assumptions that appear necessary if we are to maintain even a minimally intelligible and explicable view of the world and our place in it. Among such beliefs would be included our assumption that the world exists independently (to some extent) of our perception of it, that the causal relationships that have held in the past will continue to hold in the future, that other people possess states of conscious awareness, that we are the same person from day to day, that logical deductions are correct (e.g., black cats are indeed black), and so forth.

The basic nature of such beliefs is revealed in developmental research that has shown that abstruse but central aspects of our folk model of mind develop as early as 3 or 4 (see Wellman & Gelman, 1992; and Gopnik, 1993, for reviews). For example, by the age of 4 children appear to understand that people respond to the outside world in terms of their beliefs rather than the world itself (i.e., they understand the difference between true and false beliefs).

In one commonly used experimental task, children are required to predict how a deceptive object will be perceived by others (e.g., a candy box full of pencils) or vice-versa. Three-year-old children who have themselves observed that the candy box contains pencils, for example, consistently reported that other children will believe that the candy box contains pencils prior to examining the contents. Moreover, as Gopnik (1993) pointed out, this error is robust, occurring in many variations of the basic paradigm. For example, even when other children are observed as surprised when they discover pencils in the candy box, the attribution that the other children believed the box contained pencils is maintained. By age 4, however, children seemed to have mastered this kind of problem and other tasks that turn on an understanding that people have representations (i.e., beliefs) about the world that may be true or false—an awesome achievement that appears mundane to us only because of its apparent banality.

Asking ordinary folk to justify such beliefs (e.g., that there is a world outside their immediate awareness, or that people apart from themselves have feelings and thoughts), typically produces laughter or a refusal to take such questions seriously (if you don't believe this try it). It also produces incredulity that some grown men and women (i.e., philosophers) spend lifetimes trying to answer such questions. Indeed, the problem of how to justify such basic beliefs has been a major area of concern in philosophy from Plato and Aristotle onward.

It takes relatively little analysis to understand the difficulty in providing some sort of ultimate justification for such beliefs. Consider, for example, how we might justify the belief that other people possess states of conscious awareness (the so-called other-mind problem). The skeptic argues that we cannot possibly know, or ever adduce evidence, that other people have private experiences, because it is logically impossible to observe or experience such phenomena. One initial come-back to such an argument might be that we have at least one case where we have observed a correlation between internal experiences, such as pain, and behavior; namely, our own. The skeptic can easily counter this, however, by pointing out that we never possess even one single case where we can claim to have correctly inferred another person's mental experience from his or her behavior—to do that we would need to have observed another's mental state, and that we cannot do. Hence, we can never know whether what is true of us is true for others. The logical conclusion to the skeptic's arguments, if pressed to the limit, is solipsism—the belief that the self is the only center of conscious awareness in the Universe.

A similar problem arises when we attempt to justify our belief that the causal relationships that have held in the past will continue to operate in the future—the famous problem of induction. As Hume (1777/1962) pointed out, we cannot rescue the situation by positing some general principle that nature is (roughly) consistent, for that is assuming what we have been called on to justify. Hume's apparently feeble answer was that we are simply in the habit of assuming that the world is consistent—a solution that appears to provide no justification whatsoever. Why should the Universe continue in the same vein as in the past? Where is it written that causal laws may not change, that pigs cannot fly, or that the Universe will not suddenly become a random mess?

For my last example, consider the basic principles of logic. Again, how can such principles be justified? What do we say to a person who rejects the proposition that "black cats are black," or does not accept that accepting the truth of the premises and the logic of an argument obliges one to accept the conclusion? An initial reaction may be that such a person does not understand what he or she is rejecting. But it is conceivable that even when we have satisfied ourselves that this super-skeptic does indeed understand the rules, and may even admit to their intuitive appeal, he or she may continue to demand some powerful justification that it appears is difficult or impossible to deliver.

One answer to this general problem runs as follows. These fundamental beliefs allow people to formulate a roughly intelligible model of the world. The beliefs are basic because they allow explanatory superstructures to be erected that allow us to explain and predict the world—hence, they are necessary propositional conditions for developing plausible models of the way the world operates.

Simple thought experiments allow us to test these assertions. For example, imagine suspending your belief that other people are sentient beings like yourself, that they have beliefs and intentions and feelings, and proceed to act as if other people were automata (a variant of solipsism). One might well find oneself being relocated into a psychiatric hospital. Indeed, there is a delusional category known as Cotard's syndrome, which is similar to solipsism—the sufferer believes that nothing exists except self, and feels immortal.

Moreover, the intriguing suggestion has been made, with accompanying evidence (Baron-Cohen, 1990; Baron-Cohen, Leslie, & Frith, 1985), that there exist other living examples of this particular thought experiment in the form of the condition known as autism. Autistic children seem unable to form proper relationships, and evince a profound disorder in understanding and coping with others. It has often been observed that they appear to treat people and objects alike. Baron-Cohen argued that these problems are based on a failure to develop a theory of other people's minds and an associated impairment in the use of everyday mentalistic psychology. Autistics, for example, can reason as well as other children about physical causality but fail to appropriately attribute mental states to others, such as beliefs.

To swap to another thought experiment, imagine seriously sustaining doubt in daily life over the consistency of the social or physical world—"Will this floor hold me up?" "Will my car still be there?" "Will the car start?" "Will my friends suddenly change wholesale their personalities and attitudes?" "Will my legs hold me up?" "Will my husband still love me tomorrow?" Such doubts would obviously be almost impossible to maintain in everyday life. To be sure, inconsistencies of this sort do exist, but against a backdrop of relative invariance. Inconsistencies or failures of prediction are invariably explained by assuming a stable causal infrastructure. In short, the conclusion is resisted that such changes are occurring in a random, inexplicable, or unpredictable fashion. Without assuming, practically speaking, a reasonably predictable and orderly world, we would all become paralyzed with doubt.

Unlike the earlier beliefs examined then, there is a natural presumption that psychology should embrace this class of fundamental commonsense beliefs. It might be thought that I have just committed myself to a theory of knowledge known as foundationalism. This stance, usually associated with the philosophy of science, proposes that the rationale for scientific ways of proceeding are rooted in basic laws or beliefs that are absolutely true. I touch on this issue in chapter 5, but give an account of my general position here to avoid misunderstanding.

The approach I favor to science is that no rule, principle, method, theory, or belief is sacrosanct—every aspect is, in principle, open to revision or abandonment. However, any general scientific system of thought will contain certain fundamental beliefs or principles that will not be capable of justification by reference to other elements in that system. Of course, an attempt to rescue the situation could be made by appealing to a justification from another system of thought, such as a set of religious beliefs. Bishop Berkeley, for example, posited that we can be certain of the existence and permanence of the external world because God was permanently and omnisciently perceiving it. However, one then runs into the danger of infinite regress, because the same kind of justification can be demanded for each new rationale in turn.

Now, these arguments presented in terms of the severe and unpalatable consequences of not going along with belief in other minds, or accepting that the Universe is (roughly) consistent over time, might be considered both plausible and powerful, and they are. However, such arguments still rest on the implicit acceptance of other basic rules or beliefs, such as the need for logical consistency. Moreover, even if it meant going mad or having madness attributed to one by others, it would still be possible for someone to choose that course on "rational" grounds.

Finally, it is possible that such basic beliefs may be challenged or subtly altered by a specific theory or approach in science. Indeed, this has already happened. Radical behaviorism, for example, sought to eliminate mental expressions from psychology and instead viewed people as organisms that were controlled by the environment—in this approach people are seen as mindless (both self and others). And, within physics, quantum mechanic's postulation of an inherent level of indeterminacy in the subatomic world, has at least called into question our presumptions concerning the causal consistency of the world. Now it is true that such theories have become embroiled in dispute (both in philosophical and scientific circles), precisely because they appear to transgress fundamental commonsense dictates. Nevertheless, such scientific developments illustrate the point that in science nothing is sacred, no matter how self-evident or commonsensical it may appear.

To summarize, the view I am presenting is that all systems of thought will of necessity contain fundamental propositions that cannot be justified—at some point these propositions will need to be accepted as axiomatic. On the other hand, it cannot be stated with certainty that we have correctly identified the appropriate bedrock assumptions, nor that the entire theoretical edifice will not some day rest on a radically different set of beliefs. I return to this general issue at several points later on, in relation to models of scientific thought and whether the theories and beliefs implicit in folk psychology should be part of a mature scientific psychology. For now I turn to the second major category of commonsense psychological thought previously described—folk psychology as underlying process and structure.

FOLK PSYCHOLOGY AS A SHARED WAY OF THINKING

This aspect of commonsense theorizing I understand as consisting of the underlying shared cognitive structures and processes involved in the generation of beliefs, judgments, and behavior. Along with fundamental commonsense beliefs, this component is a hidden part of the folk psychological iceberg, in that people almost certainly have only hazy and incomplete explicit knowledge about the underlying nature of their own commonsensical theories.

Cognitive and social psychologists are often focused on this level of analysis, and typically set up general cognitive models that describe and explain cognitive schemata and processes related to a broad range of human behavior and performance. Such models are usually abstract and do not necessarily deal with the content of particular judgments or behaviors.

However, descriptions of cognitive structure and process vary in terms of their generality and, hence, applicability to different domains of psychological phenomena. Some cognitive models are set up as global descriptions of the basic human cognitive architecture. At this level, there are currently two competing general models in cognitive science. The first, and more traditional account, known as the computational or information processing approach, assumes that cognitive processing takes place in stages (Massaro & Cowan, 1993). Memorial processes, for example, are broken down into acquisition, storage and retrieval stages. Storage, in turn, is divided into short-term (or working memory) versus long-term storage. The fundamental aim is to trace how information progresses through the cognitive system from stimulus to response.

The principal competitor to an information processing account, which has emerged more recently, is known as connectionism (Smolensky, 1988). Connectionist models consist of massive networks of parallel computing elements that directly connect the stimulus (or input) to the response (or output). There are no processing stages, and serial processing is eliminated.

Attempts to adjudicate between these cognitive accounts is well beyond the scope of this book, although I attempt a more thorough analysis of connectionism later in chapter 7, where I consider the arguments of some philosophers that a connectionist account is inconsistent with a folk theory of mind. The point I wish to make here is that models of cognitive structure and process that operate at this fundamental and global level, embrace every kind of psychological phenomena from vision, to language learning, to deciding which restaurant to eat in.

However, at a more fine-grained level, domain-specific models of cognition have been advanced for a wide array of human skills or judgments, including the kinds of social judgments and beliefs that would normally be defined in terms of common sense or folk psychology. To give an example, I will take one of the most influential theories within social psychology over the last few decades, known as attribution theory, which deals with how laypeople explain behavior. The classic attribution models of Heider (1958), Kelley (1967), and Weiner (1986) all assume that what matters is not the content of the causal attribution, but where the attribution lies along a handful of content-free causal dimensions such as stability, locus of attribution, and perceived controllability (Ross & Fletcher, 1985).

What is known as the standard attributional theory, derived from the classic attributional accounts, has been usefully applied to several domains in social psychology including gender differences (Deaux, 1984), models of depression (Abramson, Seligman, & Teasdale, 1978), ethnocentrism (Fletcher & Ward, 1988), and close relationships (Fletcher & Fincham, 1991). The central idea behind the standard attributional model is that attributions function to maintain previously held beliefs, theories, or dispositions. For example, with respect to relationships, the basic idea is that people in happy relationships make attributions that maximize the favorable implications of positive behavior, but minimize the implications of negative behavior: Conversely, those in unhappy relationships adopt the opposite pattern of attributions in relation to positive and negative behaviors respectively. For example, a man in a happy relationship is likely to explain his partner's gift of flowers with a stable, internal, and global cause (e.g., she is a sensitive, caring person), but attribute his partner's insensitive remark to an unstable, externally located, and specific cause (e.g., she didn't have much sleep last night). In contrast, a man in an unhappy relationship is more likely to attribute the gift of flowers to an unstable, externally located, and specific cause (e.g., she has had a rare win on the horses), and to attribute the cutting remark to a stable, internal, and global cause (e.g., she is an insensitive bad-tempered person). The two sets of attributions can be described as *relationship-positive* and *relationship-negative*, respectively.

Hence, it can be seen that on this account, existing levels of relationship satisfaction are maintained, regardless of whether positive or negative interactive behavior is produced. This feature is linked to a central tenet in classic attribution theory; namely, that lay dispositional theories, judgments, or knowledge structures are inherently resistant to change. This tenet is hardly surprising if one considers the nightmarish alternative in which our partner and relationship judgments would shift according to every nuance and change in behavior. Attributions can, thus, be viewed as one powerful means by which the relative permanence of lay relationship models are protected against the apparently contrary and shifting behavioral evidence that is part and parcel of the typical intimate relationship.

A good deal of research has supported the validity of the standard attributional model, using a range of investigative procedures including techniques that assess the spontaneous occurrence of attributions (rather than being directly elicited by the experimenter's questions), as well as both cross-sectional and longitudinal designs (for reviews see Bradbury & Fincham, 1990; Fletcher & Fincham, 1991; and Fletcher & Fitness, 1993). The research in close relationship contexts, as well as the voluminous body of attributional research in other social domains (for reviews see Hewstone, 1989; Ross & Fletcher, 1985), support the proposition that these attributional dimensions possess psychological reality, and are not just explanatory fictions. This is perhaps not surprising, given that without the possession of such content-free knowledge structures it is difficult to see how people could ever generalize rules from one domain to another (even if such a process is difficult or flawed).

THE CONTENT AND COGNITIVE STRUCTURE
OF FOLK PSCYHOLOGY

In this section, I give a general account of how shared beliefs (the content of folk psychology) and shared cognitive structures (the abstract structure of folk psychology) are related. Understanding the way in which these two elements are connected in the form of folk psychological knowledge structures, I argue, helps answer a set of difficult questions concerning the overlap and differences between idiosyncratic and commonsense cognition.

The general relations between the content and cognitive structure of folk psychology are shown in Fig. 2.1. As can be seen, this figure allows for all three categories to both overlap and retain their separate identities. The top category represents folk psychology as a way of thinking, and includes both very general

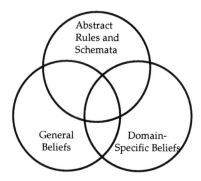

FIG. 2.1.   The content and structure of folk psychology.

cognitive structures or systems, and also more domain-specific schemata, such as the attribution schemata previously described. The general beliefs category includes the sort of culturally derived beliefs previously described, including proverbs, and fundamental or widely held beliefs. The specific beliefs category is meant to represent an individuals' particular sets of beliefs concerning individuals or groups. This way of presenting folk psychology, then, moves from the most general and shared level to the least shared and most specific level.

I again use an example from research and theorizing in close-relationship cognition to briefly illustrate certain features of this general account (see Fletcher & Fitness, 1993; Fletcher & Thomas, in press). In the close-relationship domain, the abstract rules and schemata category consists of global abstract rules and schemata that apply to social behavior generally, as well as particular cognitive structures that apply specifically to close-relationship contexts. I previously gave an example of the standard attributional theory that describes the kind of abstract schemata that would fit into this category.

The general beliefs category would include beliefs that individuals have concerning how intimate, romantic relationships function. There is good evidence that people select such beliefs from a culturally derived list of factors that specify the important causes of successful or unsuccessful intimate relationships. In developing a scale to measure such beliefs, Fletcher and Kininmonth (1992), attempted to describe this general set of beliefs by asking university-based and nonuniversity-based samples to write down all the factors that they believed would produce a successful loving romantic relationship (either married or unmarried). The 18-belief taxonomy subsequently derived from these statements are shown in Table 2.1, with representative examples of the statements provided. The factor labels (Intimacy, External Factors, Passion, Individuality) are derived from a factor analysis of a scale based on this qualitative analysis, and suggest that these beliefs can be categorized according to a simpler higher order conceptual structure.

In accordance with Fig. 2.1, there is also evidence that the kind of general beliefs and ideals people have concerning intimate relationships in general terms, are strongly related to their relationship-specific models or theories. First, it is clear

TABLE 2.1
Factor Labels, Individual Beliefs, and Example Items From the Relationship Belief Scale

Intimacy

Trust	There must be complete honesty between partners
Respect	Mutual respect is the foundation for the best relationships
Communication	People must always listen to their partners' underlying messages
Coping	Conflict in a relationship must be confronted directly
Support	In the best relationships, partners work hard at satisfying each other's needs
Acceptance	In happy relationships, partners totally accept one another
Love	Close relationships cannot work without love
Friendship	Your partner should be your best friend
Compromise	Both partners must make sacrifices in relationships

External Factors

Personal security	If both partners come from secure and caring families the relationship is much more likely to succeed
Important others	Having friends in common cements relationships
Finance	Money is as important as love in a relationship
Commonality	Partners must share the same beliefs and values
Children	Having children brings couples together

Passion

Sex	Without good sex, relationships do not survive
Vitality	Relationships must be exciting

Individuality

Independence	Each partner has a right to absolute personal privacy
Equity	Men and woman must equally share household chores

that accounts or theories of specific relationships are woven out of the same conceptual materials as are the general theories (see Fletcher & Fitness, in press). Second, in a continuing program of research Fletcher and his colleagues have found good evidence that judgments of an on-going relationship (How successful is it? Will it last? Are we well matched?) are generated, in part, by the match between how the current relationship is perceived, and prior beliefs or theories concerning the ideal relationship or what factors produce a successful relationship (Fletcher & Kininmonth, 1992; Fletcher, Rosanowski, & Fitness, 1994; Fletcher, Simpson, & Thomas, 1995).

There is no difficulty in general terms in understanding where general beliefs or lay theories about close relationships come from. We are bombarded daily with a profusion of information about intimate close relationships in pop songs, agony columns, self-help books, romantic novels, TV plays, sitcoms, advertisements, stage plays, movies, and so on. From such sources, then, a loose but widely shared folk "theory" has emerged that specifies the factors that produce successful intimate relationships.

However, such a theory does not rigidly specify local-level theories that people hold concerning specific relationships. Based on a background of personal experiences and observations, personality characteristics, not to mention the unique characteristics that all relationships possess, people appear to select from and modify this general-level theory when applying it to specific relationships (see Fletcher & Fitness, in press).

Moreover, even at the level of general beliefs and theories, strong individual differences exist. For example, people possess strongly varying beliefs concerning the importance of passion or sex in producing successful relationships (Fletcher & Kininmonth, 1992). Some believe that sex is a central element in determining whether close relationships work. Others believe passion (hot or cold) to be of little account.

Individual differences also exist for the abstract rules or schema that can be described in a content-free fashion. Take, for example, the standard attribution model already described that postulates certain causal dimensions as critical (rather than the specific content of the causes), including internality, globality, and stability. There is good evidence from attributional models of depression (e.g., Seligman, 1991), that there are important individual differences in how people characteristically use such dimensions in explaining negative events in their lives; to wit, those who are prone to depression, compared to those that are not, appear to favor explaining negative events with causes that are internal, global, and stable (e.g., I am insecure).

In general terms, then, as the level of description of everyday cognition proceeds from the general to the specific, the more cognition appears to become personalized and idiosyncratic. However, even at the most local level, it is clear that an individual's lay beliefs or judgments are derived from, and conditioned by, sets of widely shared cognitive schemata and associated beliefs.

Interestingly, one of the key differences between folk psychology and scientific psychology sometimes advanced is that folk theories are irredeemably local in their application in contrast to scientific theories that are inescapably general. As Wilkes (1993) said, "George wants to know why his daughter Georgina has become a skinhead, a mathemetics professor, or a born-again Christian, rather than why teenagers are tempted to become skinheads, to take up mathematics, or to get waylaid by fundamentalism" (p. 171).

This argument is fallacious. First, scientists are often very interested in detailing and explaining local events—particular volcanos, earthquakes, fossils, super novae, suicides, riots, wars, and so forth. Scientists, including psychologists, are continuously moving between the specific and the general, because both kinds of analysis support and inform one another. Understanding local or specific events can raise or help answer questions at the general theoretical level, whereas one major rationale for building general theories is to improve prediction, explanation, and control of specific events. Second, there is compelling empirical evidence, a few examples of which I have cited, that laypeople are in fact interested in, and build general theories about, the kind of events that Wilkes claimed they do not.

WHAT IS NOT FOLK PSYCHOLOGY?

My analysis of folk psychology so far may appear benign, and it is certainly consistent with the work of previous psychologists who have chanced their arms with this domain (Farr, 1981; Furnham, 1983; Wegner & Vallacher, 1981). However, Kelley (1992) suggested that including "process" as part of folk psychology is problematic because this step brings all of cognitive psychology into the definition of common sense, and is, thus, over inclusive. Kelley certainly raised a definitional issue of importance here. However, provided folk psychology is only allowed to include those processes and structures that are intimately involved in the generation of folk beliefs or social judgments, then this problem is averted, because vast reaches of cognitive psychology are then excluded, including the study of vision, hearing, asocial problem solving, and so forth.

Moreover, there are problems here concerning the meaning of *process*. As part of this term, I am inclined to include the underlying postulated cognitive structures or schemata, as well as some idea of the way in which relevant components interact with one another. Indeed, in practice I do not think it possible to do one without the other, even if it is in an embryonic fashion. Kelley (1992) himself included underlying cognitive structures as part of common-sense psychological theory, and, hence, I think also dealt with process (or at any rate what I take process to refer to).

Another issue concerns the extent to which the individual's psychological theories are exhausted by folk formulations. The answer to this question depends, in part, on one's overall theoretical bent. The more extreme versions of social constructionism, such as those proposed by Gergen (1985), Harré (1989), and Shotter (1984), propose that social behavior and cognition are completely determined by the structural properties of the collective, and by the norms and rules imbedded in social interaction. Such an approach implies that every personal belief and way of thinking, every aspect of an individual's social cognition, will be a shared part of one's culture (i.e., psychological common sense). Mainstream social psychology and cognition is attacked, according to this approach, as overly individualistic, as missing the central nature of human cognition and behavior—its social imbededness.

Like many other (mainstream) social psychologists, I believe this attack has a point. Contemporary social cognition, in particular, tends to be "social" in only the minimal sense that it is concerned with social judgments such as stereotyping and trait attributions. Social cognition research seldom deals with social or interactive behavior, and almost exclusively investigates intrapsychic processes in laboratory-based settings with verbal materials.

So, I would endorse the claim that social psychology and social cognition needs to become more concerned with social behavior. However, such a declaration does not imply that a radical social constructionism is correct. I have already argued that widely shared theories influence or constrain even apparently idiosyncratic lay cognition or theories. However, this does not entail that an individual's cognitions or theories are fully determined by the wider social order. Indeed, the empirical research shows only too clearly that there are characteristic differences between general socially derived theories and beliefs, and the more idiosyncratic beliefs and theories held by individuals. Moreover, as already noted, there are strong individual differences in the extent to which individuals adhere to widely shared beliefs or theories. A radical social constructionism, in my view, presents an oversocialized view of human cognition and behavior that neither allows for nor explains an individual's cognition or social behavior that is, to some extent, idiosyncratic (Fletcher, in press-a).

In summary, I believe it is an open question to what extent an individual's social schemata and beliefs are a shared and direct product of social forces. As befits my social psychological biases, I am inclined to think a good deal of our everyday social thinking is linked to the wider social forces at work, but it also seems clear that individuals can and do reflectively examine socially derived beliefs and social norms, and may challenge or alter such beliefs as a result of such private scrutiny. The extent to which such critical and individualistic cognition occurs will presumably vary tremendously from culture to culture and across individuals within cultures. In open Western-style democracies, where individualism is encouraged and rational scrutiny of societal norms is commonplace, it seems to me peculiar to view people only as ciphers in a wider social structure, as units proceeding in lockstep according to sets of norms and rules for behavior. Society creates individuals, but individuals also create society. A radical social constructionism, it seems to me, leaves out the second part of the equation and fails to properly consider the unique and strange intellectual powers of human beings that evolution has thrown up in the last second (so to speak) of the earth's history.

CONCLUSION

Folk psychology can be regarded as providing a rich cultural and cognitive resource from which individuals mold their own personalized lay theories and beliefs. In this chapter I attempted to provide a componential analysis of folk psychology. There remain important issues concerning the nature of folk psychology that I have not as yet touched on, the most important perhaps being the extent to which folk psychology consists of theoretical knowledge (qua science). However, this issue, among others, is addressed later in the book. In the next chapter, I focus on an important domain of common sense: the folk psychology of the mind.

Chapter 3
Folk Psychology of the Mind

As previously discussed, most of the philosophical treatments of folk psychology have (rightly or wrongly) defined folk psychology in terms of the mental realm. Indeed, there is no doubt that commonsense theories of the mind are a central component of folk psychology. In this chapter, therefore, I provide a brief description of the folk model of mind.

Because we all use folk psychological theories does not necessarily mean that we can easily describe their contents or how they function, any more than we can explain how our brains work because we all use them to think with. Various attempts have been made to chart the outlines of folk theories of the mind. Philosophers have often attempted to describe the important features of commonsense theorizing, typically using conceptual analysis of everyday language (e.g., Anscombe, 1963; Searle, 1980). A few psychologists, too, have chanced their arm in providing general descriptions of folk theory, but have usually based their work on the empirical analysis of questionnaire responses (e.g., D'Andrade, 1987; Rips & Conrad, 1989).

In addition, psychologists have examined folk theories as they apply to specific domains, such as emotions, close relationships, lay explanations, personality traits, and so forth. Such empirical investigations provide illuminating evidence concerning how folk psychology theory functions in general terms. I refer to some of this research in due course.

The lay model of mind, depicted in Fig. 3.1, is derived from a variety of psychological and philosophical sources. In the following sections I illustrate and provide evidence for the following general propositions. First, folk theory assumes that experiences, knowledge, and tendencies, are stored in the form of dispositions. Second, such dispositions are seen as functionally distinct entities, although intimately connected to one another and to cognitive process. Third, folk theories of the mind are inextricably intertwined with behavior, both in terms of how behavior is explained and how behavior is perceived and interpreted.

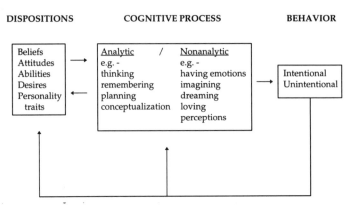

FIG. 3.1.   The folk model of the mind.

In the first section of this chapter I briefly describe the different elements depicted in Fig. 3.1, and in the second part I discuss how the elements are combined to form coherent folk psychological theories.

Dispositions

Beliefs.   Beliefs are often implicitly involved in other kinds of dispositions, such as attitudes and desires, for example, that I like Mary (an attitude) implicitly entails that I believe Mary is a person. In addition, we have many beliefs that refer to other elements in the overall folk model, or refer to other beliefs (so-called second-order beliefs), for example, I believe that I am ambitious, that I want more money, that I liked Jim, that I am musical, that I intended to eat the whole cake, and that I once believed in God. That is, we have beliefs about our attitudes, our abilities, our personalities, our behavior, our emotions, and so forth. Beliefs can be intimately connected to overt behavior (e.g., I believe I will pass this test), or unconnected to behavior (I believe that I am thinking). They can refer to the self or involve attributions to other individuals or groups (unlike abilities, desires, and personality traits that only concern the self). In summary, the set of belief dispositions is amorphous and uncountably huge if we include every conceivable kind of explicit and implicit belief that a given person might hold.

Belief attributions are the most global, and perhaps the most fundamental cognitive attribution in folk psychology. In folk psychology, beliefs have causal status often being cited as causes for behavior or other mental states. Yet, beliefs can also remain supine, without being expressed in observable behavior. For example, I can believe that Fred is a fool, but never express such a belief in any observable way.

Attitudes.   Attitudes involve affective and cognitive elements wrapped up in some sort of evaluative judgment of a target. Examples would include liking ice cream or disliking a person, strongly believing that capital punishment is bad, or hating the president. Attitudes seem to require a target (either inside or outside the person—one can have attitudes toward oneself), and also an evaluative element. All attitudes implicitly or explicitly contain beliefs, but only those beliefs that have evaluative components would normally be counted as attitudes. For example, my belief that Frank is my neighbor is not an attitude because it contains no evaluation of Frank or neighbors. However, if I believe that Frank is an intrusive and unreliable neighbor than this belief constitutes an attitude.

Abilities. The attribution of abilities is common in everyday life. Studies that have content-coded the kinds of attributions spontaneously produced by people for success or failure in sporting, academic, and social settings have consistently found that dispositional attributions of ability are one of the most common class of explanations (Weiner, 1985). Ability attributions vary in terms of their globality. Some attributions are global, such as smart or dumb, whereas others are more specific, such as possessing artistic or mathematical ability.

Desires. Desires bring most explicitly into play the crucial commonsense idea that much of human behavior is goal-directed, and under the control of the individual. To have a desire for something implies that, all being equal, an individual will strive to attain some goal. The stronger the desire, the stronger the inclination.

Personality Traits. Many personality traits describe simple, observable patterns of behavior, such as talkative, punctual, or untidy. Other personality traits refer to both the cognitive and behavioral realm, and include references to cognition or affect and behavior; for example, tolerant, warm, independent, stubborn, confident, daydreamer, and insecure. The importance of such constructs is reflected in their prevalence in our language: Of the 18,000 person-descriptive terms Allport and Odbert (1936) found in a standard English dictionary, 4,504 described stable personality dispositions (Eiser, 1983).

The links between behavior and personality traits are variable in folk psychology, depending on the nature of the trait. In general, traits that are more closely connected to behavior (e.g., assertive, cheerful) are judged by naive raters as relatively easy to observe and as easier to accurately attribute to others. In contrast, traits that are more abstract and more closely associated with the mental realm (e.g., anxious, introspective, insecure), are judged as relatively hard to observe, and as more difficult to accurately attribute to others (see Funder & Dobroth, 1987; Rothbart & Park, 1986). Indeed, Funder and Dobroth found that laypeople are indeed more accurate in the judgments of their peers when rating behavioral traits as compared to the more cognitive traits.

Cognitive Process

The description of this section of the folk model is principally derived from the research by Rips and Conrad (1989) who first obtained lists of mental activities from a sample of naive raters, then had other samples make various ratings on the list of mental activities that were derived from the original set of free responses. The central point I make here is that mental activities in folk psychology seem to revolve around what Rips and Conrad termed an *analytic versus nonanalytic dimension*. Analytic cognitive processes seem to be cognitive in orientation and subject to control by the individual. Nonanalytic processes are more experiential in nature, more affective, and less under the control of the individual.

Behavior

The way in which human behavior is perceived, described, and explained by ordinary folk is intimately entangled with the folk psychology of the mind. For example, one of the key dimensions in the perception and interpretation of behavior is the degree to which the behavior is perceived as intentional or controlled by the individual. As pointed out by many philosophers and psychologists, behavior is typically not perceived simply as a series of events, but is often automatically filtered through the prism of our folk psychological theories.

When observing people baking a cake, shopping at the supermarket, doing the gardening, washing the dishes, reading a book, and so forth, it is simply assumed that these behaviors are carried out intentionally, and are underpinned by dispositions such as desires, beliefs, and abilities. Unintentional behaviors, also, are often linked to underlying dispositions or cognitive activities. For example, unintentionally forgetting one's partner's birthday could readily be explained in terms of one's attitude (lack of love), or a personality trait (insensitivity), or an emotional state (anger). Spilling one's tea might also be explained in terms of a trait like clumsiness or a cognitive activity like daydreaming.

Heider (1958) postulated that the layperson uses three criteria in assessing intentionality: equifinality, local causality, and exertion. *Equifinality* refers to the fact that intentional action is goal-directed, implying that people will use a variety of strategies to attain a goal. *Local causality* is established when the actor is seen as the originator of the behavior. Finally, *perceived exertion* is an indicator that an intention is present. One point to note is that these criterial behaviors are easily observable. We so habitually and automatically perceive everyday actions, such as baking cakes, as intentional or goal-directed, it is difficult to imagine how they can be described or perceived in other ways. Fundamental concepts, like intentionality, are difficult to prise off the world.

However, none of this means that the distinction between intentional and unintentional behavior is unambiguous. Indeed, the distinction is probably best represented as a dimension, in that behaviors or actions can be a mixture of both intentional and unintentional elements, and individual behaviors can be perceived as moderately intentional. Moreover, there are many occasions when it is difficult to tell whether a behavior was intentional or unintentional. The fate of a defendant in a murder trial often hangs on whether he or she is judged by the jury as intending to murder the victim.

Political reputations, too, can hang on the perceived intentionality of a behavior. While I was writing this section of the book, a well-known Republican raised a furor when, in a radio address, he referred to a well-known Democrat, whose name was Barney Frank, as Barney Fag. Barney Frank happens to be self-proclaimed homosexual. The Republican later apologized, explained it as a slip of the tongue, and stressed his lack of prejudice toward homosexuals. Other politicians (Democrats of course) claimed his slip of the tongue was intentional and revealed his true attitudes. Barney Frank pronounced that he accepted that the act was not intentional, but nevertheless said it revealed the perpetrator's latent homophobia.

As noted in the previous chapter, the area of research in psychology that has most explicitly examined lay explanations for human behavior is known as attribution theory. Indeed, attribution theory has spawned hundreds of experiments, and has been one of the dominant domains in social psychology since the 1970s. The body of attributional research is consistent with the general account offered here (for reviews see Hewstone, 1989; Ross & Fletcher, 1985). Specifically, lay causal schemata appear to be organized around dimensions that I have already suggested are central to folk psychology; namely, stability and controllability.

Mental Connections

The principal point I stress in this section is that elements in the folk model of mind are typically connected to one another in complex ways, a feature that is clearly apparent when analyzing the nature of lay interpretation and explanation of experiences and behavior. The fact that more than one kind of mental disposition is typically needed to adequately explain a given behavior has often been pointed out by philosophers. For example, to explain why Mary crossed the road, we may cite a belief (she believed there was a shop selling cigarettes on the other side), and a desire (Mary wanted to buy some cigarettes).

There is also striking evidence that in the process of attributing cognitive processes, states, or activities to themselves or others, laypeople will base such attributions on complex schemata that involve putative causal and semantic relationships among several components in the folk model of mind. The lay attribution of emotions to self or others is a case in point (see Fehr & Baldwin, in press; Fitness, in press). For example, Fitness and Fletcher (1993) examined the knowledge structures associated with four emotions in relationship contexts: love, hate, anger, and jealousy. In Study 1 of this research, 160 married men and women completed a series of open-ended and Likert-scaled questions concerning these emotions as they were recently experienced in their relationships. Four distinct but overlapping prototypes of each emotion were subsequently assembled from these accounts that, apart from the raw experience itself (the qualia), included characteristics of the instigating events, other emotions experienced, behavioral urges, control strategies, the duration of the event, partner's reactions, self-behavior, as well as a series of judgments along various appraisal dimensions.

For example, the following thumbnail sketches for love and anger were produced (Fitness & Fletcher, 1993):

> Subjects feeling love for their spouses felt warm and relaxed and were thinking positively; they wanted to be close to their spouses and usually expressed their feelings to them, both verbally and nonverbally. In addition, love-eliciting events were appraised as pleasant, good for the relationship, and involving little effort. The cause of love was appraised as being global rather than specific. Subjects felt calm and relaxed before the eliciting event, and their partner's reactions were overwhelmingly positive.

> Subjects feeling angry with their spouses believed they had been treated unfairly; they felt a good deal of muscle tension along with being hot and bothered and wanted to express their feelings (which they typically did, both verbally and nonverbally). Despite the short-lived nature of the anger incident, subjects tended to feel tense or depressed afterward. In contrast with hate and jealousy, anger events were appraised as predictable, and ... subjects perceived themselves as to have more control over the situation. Anger events were also appraised as being the partner's fault, compared with a low partner responsibility rating for jealousy. (pp. 948–949)

In a second study (Fitness & Fletcher, 1993), a different sample of married men and women wrote fictional accounts of stereotypical accounts of the same four emotions. As predicted, the results showed a considerable degree of similarity with those from the prior study, suggesting that both accounts were being drawn from the same knowledge base. And, finally, in Study 3, information derived from the prior studies (including descriptions of the qualia, behavior, partner reactions, control strategies, and the instigating event) was supplied in varying amounts to a new sample of naive subjects, but without mentioning the emotion itself. The results showed that the more information was provided, the more accurately could subjects identify the particular emotion being described when asked to choose the correct emotion from a list of four negative and four positive emotions (hate, anger, jealousy, worry, love, happiness, relief, and pride).

For example, when supplied with a stripped-down ambiguous description of a "love" event (e.g., Patricia and Derek are on holiday together. Patricia goes way over budget when she buys Derek an expensive piece of pottery. What is Derek feeling?), subjects correctly picked the emotion of love at close to chance levels (under 20% accuracy). When information along abstract appraisal dimensions was added to this scenario, the accuracy rate improved to 52%. In the scenario already described, this extra information consisted of the following: Derek isn't at all surprised, for he believes it is typical of Patricia to do things like this. After all, she is a very generous person. Derek finds her behavior easy to understand and predictable.

In the condition in which the most comprehensive information was provided, but still without identifying the emotion itself, accuracy rates improved to 69% overall. For example, when subjects were provided with the following kind of scenario, they correctly identified the emotion as jealousy 80% of the time:

Rob does not enjoy squash, so Wendy decides to play with a work colleague. Rob is feeling sick and agitated. He knows it's not Wendy's fault that she enjoys squash and he doesn't, but he feels she could easily give the game up rather than play with someone else. He wants to tell Wendy how he fells about the situation, but spends most of his time brooding instead. He can't understand what is going on; its not like Wendy to act this way. When she returns from her first game, Rob acts coldly and withdraws physically and emotionally from her.

The findings from this research are consistent with the general research literature and support a picture of lay emotional attributions as embedded in relatively complex but inherently fuzzy prototypes that have a scriptlike quality. To quote Fitness (in press):

> Each script is characterized by particular kinds of emotion-eliciting scenarios, or core relational themes. Thus, when we learn that Paul is angry with Susan, we can assume that Susan has offended Paul in some way, or has thwarted his plans or expectations, and that her behavior may or may not have been intentional, but that Paul apparently believes it is. In addition, and like all good stories, people's emotion scripts comprise details of characteristic physiological symptoms (Paul is probably feeling hot and bothered), behavioral urges that may or may not be acted on (Paul may want to punish Susan), immediate behavioral responses (Paul may yell at Susan), control strategies (Paul may go for a walk to cool off), and likely partner responses (Susan may apologize or retaliate).

The work from the emotion field is also consistent with a vast body of evidence from social psychology that what applies to emotions, applies equally to all manner of self-judgments, including those that involve distinct qualia or internal experiences. Take the much-researched topic concerning the self-attribution of attitudes. The relevant body of research suggests that attitudes are firmly linked to behaviors in terms of cognitive schemata, such that people tend to infer their own attitudes from their own behavior or behavioral context, and also to use their own attitudes as cues in recall of their behavior (see Ross & Fletcher, 1985).

For example, a well-replicated finding in social psychology is that when either children or adults are rewarded for carrying out a previously enjoyable activity, their attitudes toward the activity alters in a negative direction (see Deci & Ryan, 1985). The provision of a salient and plausible external cause of their behavior (e.g., monetary reward) leads people to automatically infer that the internal cause (love of the activity) is less important: hey presto, attitude change occurs. As an example of this cognitive connection between attitude and behavior working in reverse, Ross et al. (1981) showed that changing the attitudes people held toward toothbrushing or bathing substantially altered their recall of the frequency of toothbrushing or bathing in the preceding weeks.

In summary, the self-attribution of mental states or dispositions does not appear to follow a naive introspectionist model, in which people unerringly label their internal desires, attitudes beliefs, and so forth, in some direct observational fashion. Rather, the evidence indicates that self-attribution is a theory-driven process, in much the same way as is the attribution of psychological states and dispositions to others. To be sure, the way in which we attribute internal feelings or beliefs so confidently and rapidly, may create the illusion that introspective judgment is a matter of simple and direct observation of our cognitive innards. But given the long learning history behind such attributions, their frequency of use, and the massive expertise developed concerning their use, it is hardly surprising that this should be the case. The question of whether cognitive judgments to the self are theory driven will be engaged again in the next chapter. For now, I turn briefly to the research dealing with personality attributions.

The study of how laypeople develop impressions of specific individuals also demonstrates a key point I have been making (see Fiske, 1993). That is, information about other people is rapidly and routinely organized into coherent structures in which the constituent parts are combined according to causal, semantic, and logical relations. Individuals are not merely seen as a collection of unrelated dispositions. For example, loneliness may be seen as causing depression, which, in turn, causes the person to be pessimistic and therefore unhappy (see Sedikides & Anderson, 1994).

Park (1986) had subjects provide open-ended descriptions of their peers at weekly intervals during a course in which they were participating. Over time, the descriptions became increasingly abstract and coherent, but even after the first 2-hour class, the thumbnail sketches possessed considerable internal coherence. Here is one example Park cited:

> Self-centered and domineering, Martha spends so much time assuring herself that she is the center of attention, that she forgets about the feelings of others. She is wealthy and egotistical, which makes for great fashion sense and good looks. She spends much time and takes great pride in her appearance. She is very intelligent, but classes serve only as a showcase to display her talents. She disturbs class by being loud and boisterous. (p. 910)

The close connection between lay mental attributions and descriptions of behavior has sometimes been cited as a reason for questioning the scientific status of folk psychology (e.g., Haldane, 1988). Lay explanations are scientifically unrespectable, so goes the argument, because the putative mental causes are linked too closely at the conceptual level to their effects. In "real" scientific theories, it is claimed, causes and effects are conceptually distinct.

The major problem with this argument is that what is true for folk psychology is also generally true for other scientific theories. As Churchland (1991) pointed out, in long-established scientific theories, including those in psychology, it is typically the case that descriptions of the facts to be explained are framed partly in terms of the theory itself. In behaviorism, for example, events to be explained are typically described in behavioral terms. In relativity theory or Newtonian mechanics, basic descriptive terms like force, mass, velocity, momentum, time, and space are also defined in terms of their relationships within the wider theory. Given the many centuries that folk psychology has been developing, it is hardly surprising that the folk language and theory of the mind have spilled over into folk description of behavior (and vice-versa).

CONCLUSION

Having completed at least a provisional analysis of commonsense knowledge in the last two chapters, I am now in a better position to examine more closely the relations between folk psychology and scientific psychology, the topic of the next chapter.

Chapter 4
Uses and Abuses of Folk Psychology in Scientific Psychology

This chapter deals primarily with the descriptive question of what the links are between folk psychology and scientific psychology. I postpone a thorough consideration of what the relations between the two spheres should be (a prescriptive question) to the next section of the book. In practice, the two questions are intermingled; hence, there is some inevitable straying across the boundaries.

Folk psychological knowledge and theory is used in two principal ways by psychology. The first use is based on the assumption in contemporary psychology that folk beliefs and lay psychological theories exert a substantial causal influence on judgments and behavior. Indeed, commonsense thinking is, in part, the subject matter of certain disciplines within psychology, such as social psychology and social cognition. Accordingly, social psychological models almost invariably include an account of these cognitive structures. This usage is henceforth termed *Use₁*. Second, folk psychology is often used as a resource for helping to build an overarching psychological theory that goes beyond the aims and purview of folk "theory" itself. This latter usage is termed *Use₂* (see Fletcher, in press-b).

I illustrate and expand on these two principal ways in which folk psychology is exploited in psychology. Let me build a base for this account with a few central ideas. First, note that the validity or truth value of folk psychology is not an issue when thinking of the former usage of commonsense theory (Use₁). Folk beliefs and lay theories may be completely addled, yet still exert a causal influence on subsequent thought or behavior. The common belief that men are more mathematically astute than women may well be fallacious. Nevertheless, attribution of this belief may explain why a given individual preferred to hire a man than a woman for a job that required statistical expertise. In contrast, to use folk psychology as a resource for an overarching professional psychological theory (Use₂) clearly assumes that commonsense theory is valid or at least plausible—if folk psychology

30

is a crock (as some have claimed) then this procedure will inevitably produce a flawed theory.

Second, it bears reiterating that scientific psychology, especially social psychology, needs to pay attention to folk psychology because folk theories play a causal role in producing the very behavior and cognition that social psychologists are interested in. This is a curious and important fact that decisively demarcates psychology from the other sciences. Of course, ordinary folk also have lay theories about physics and biology, and possibly even palaeontology. But the physicist, biologist, and palaeontologist are not obliged to consult such folk theories in the development of scientific theories, because such lay beliefs do not causally influence the phenomena in question (e.g., the orbits of the planets, the action of cells, or the evolutionary history of life on earth).

Third, this double-barreled role that folk psychology can play in the development of psychological theories has important and widely unrecognized implications for both psychology and the philosophy of psychology. As I argue in chapter 7, those philosophers who have pressed for the elimination of folk psychology from psychology have wrongly assumed that the sole role played in psychology by common sense is as a source for our master psychological theories (Use2), and have stunningly missed the point that even if psychology is so purged folk psychology may still form a substantial component in scientific psychological theories (Use1).

Psychologists, unfortunately, are also not without sin; namely, they frequently conflate and confuse the two functions of folk psychology, both at the methodological and theoretical level. I give some examples of this confusion and its deleterious consequences in the final section of this chapter. For now, I deal directly with the actual overlap between scientific psychology and folk psychology and attempt to put some meat on these general bones. The way in which folk psychology is imported into psychology is dealt with first, followed by a brief discursion on the reverse relation (i.e., the flow of ideas from psychology to commonsense thought).

THE INCORPORATION OF FOLK PSYCHOLOGY INTO PSYCHOLOGICAL THEORIZING

The Role of Folk Psychology as a Causal Component of Scientific Psychological Theories (Use1)

In accordance with the division between content and process described in the previous chapter, there are two major ways in which psychologists incorporate folk psychology into psychological models (in terms of Use1): as abstract content-free rules, structures, or processes, or in terms of categories or information-rich items that reflect the content of commonsense beliefs, attitudes, expectations, and the like.

As already noted, this use of folk psychology is widespread in scientific psychology, especially in social psychology and social cognition. For example, in chapter 2, I described some research by myself and my colleagues that illustrated how folk knowledge and theory concerning close relationships can be described in terms of both abstract cognitive schemata, and in terms of particular beliefs. The postulation of similar kinds of knowledge structures can also be found in the study of person memory, stereotyping, personality impressions, emotion, self-perception, persuasion, depression, gender roles, group behavior, conformity, decision making, prejudice, aggression, and so on.

The extensive use that psychologists have made of folk psychology rests on the assumption that folk theories drive, in part, both attributions to the self (such as attitudes, beliefs, and emotions) and attributions to others. It seems intuitively plausible that internal or mental attributions to others might be heavily influenced by folk theories, given that we do not have access to other people's "actual" mental or experiences. However, it could be argued that mentalistic attributions to the self are based on private introspective access, akin to pure observation rather than theoretical inference.

This latter claim has been vigorously pressed recently by Goldman (1992, 1993), who argued that folk psychological judgments are not principally driven by folk theories, a claim I now turn to.

Are Mental Attributions to the Self Theoretically Driven?   The standard view in psychology and cognitive science is that mental attributions to the self are driven, in part, by commonsensical functional theories of mind. Functionalist theories of mind locate mental attributions within a framework of goals, antecedent causes, and consequences. In other words, the plausibility of a mental attribution within folk psychology is determined by understanding how it is located within a network of causal relations to environmental triggers, other mental states or dispositions, and subsequent behavior or judgments.

Goldman's alternative to a functionalist account is a cruder introspectionist approach in which private experiences, or *qualia* as they are termed by philosophers, are directly perceived and associated with a given label or description. It is important to note here that Goldman is explicitly concerned with Use$_1$ of folk psychology; namely, the description of how folk psychology is actually constituted rather than the development of an overarching theoretical account (Use$_2$).

There are few psychologists nowadays who believe in the kind of introspectionist approach proposed by Goldman (1992) as a description of how folk psychology works, and for good reason. As Goldman recognizes, an introspectionist account becomes most problematic when mental attributions like beliefs or desires are considered, because it is not clear what qualia or internal experiences are involved in such attributions. Consider, for example, and introspectly assess the internal qualia involved in a belief like "I believe that the moon is round" as against a desire like "I would like to visit the moon," or against another belief like "I believe it is raining." The often recognized problem with such attributions is that there do not seem to be internally distinguishable qualia involved, so that one is reduced to repeating the assertions, or talking about the differences between the moon and the weather, or talking about the meaning of "beliefs" versus "desires."

However, even in cases where there appear to be clear-cut internal experiences or qualia involved, the psychological evidence shows that a simple introspectionist account is wrong as a description of how related attributions are made. For example, as described in chapter 4, the study of lay emotional attributions and attitude attributions has shown that such attributions to the self are based on a functional model, in which the nature of the underlying feeling is but one factor in determining the relevant attribution (see, e.g., Fehr & Baldwin, in press; Fitness, in press). This characteristic of mental attributions to the self has been described by Pylyshyn (1980) as one of "cognitive penetrability." That is, lay attributions of mental states or dispositions can readily be altered by manipulating information about features (such as behavior or consequences) that have a theoretical connection to the mental attribution itself. As argued by Pylyshyn, this feature of mentalistic attribution indicates that the attributions are, in part, theory driven.

In summary, it is possible to allow for the existence and operation of private experiences or perceptions, while also holding to a functional account of common-sense mental attributions. Furthermore, this approach solves some knotty problems. First, it explains how the interpretation and labeling of private experiences is tied into the language and socialization practices of the wider culture. Second, it provides a plausible way of understanding how laypeople make mental attributions to others as well as themselves. Third, it explains why (in commonsense psycho-logic), it makes sense to attribute mental states to others, even when they may deny such a self-attribution. For example, an individual may satisfy all the prototypical features of feeling angry (e.g., feeling unfairly treated, reacting with the appropriate behavioral display, feeling tense and depressed afterward, and blaming his or her partner for the problem), but deny that he or she is feeling angry. In this context, we would probably claim that the person was either acting, lying, or kidding themselves. Finally, the fact that individuals can readily feign emotions, beliefs, or attitudes, in order to attain social goals, illustrates the mastery that people have over the functional architecture of such mental attributions.

Content and Process.   In some psychological models, weight is given to both cognitive structure and process and to the content of lay cognition, which means considering the particular beliefs or social judgments that individuals hold. Indeed, it has become apparent over the last decade in social cognition that paying attention to the content of lay beliefs or attributions can lend insight into underlying cognitive schemata or process.

Take, for example, the work dealing with how ordinary folk attribute traits or dispositions. Most earlier work dealing with this process adopted the standard cognitive approach and treated dispositions as a homogeneous class. Yet the work of Reeder and his colleagues demonstrates that the underlying schemata tracking the relations between behavioral criteria and the attribution of dispositions, will differ according to the kind of disposition attributed (for a review see Reeder, 1993). Some traits (e.g., talkativeness, punctuality, etc.) appear to be associated with a straightforward frequency schema in which the strength of the attribution is directly associated with the relative frequency of behavior. There is good evidence, however, that other traits (e.g., ability and morality) are asymmetrical with respect to positive and negative behavioral criteria. For example, people confidently make extreme dishonesty attributions on the basis of one example of dishonest behavior, but make weak honesty attributions on the basis of one example of honest behavior.

Conclusion. I conclude this section with some general points concerning Use₁. First, Use₁ of folk psychology does not embrace any commitment to the truth value or scientific credibility of the relevant knowledge structures. Even if lay beliefs concerning the causes of relationship success are nonsense or folk causal theories are erroneous, in order to explain how people make judgments about close relationships, or make causal attributions, psychologists need to take such lay theories into account.

Second, Use₁ of folk psychology (unlike Use₂) is going to be restricted to those domains where folk theories actually exist. As I have already indicated, folk psychology does appear to be alive and well in areas such as social psychology and personality theory; however, folk theories may be virtually nonexistent in domains like neuropsychology, auditory perception, and language learning (more on this point later).

Third, making use of folk psychology in terms of Use₁ does not imply that the related scientific theory is restricted to folk psychology. For example, some social psychological theories explore such issues as the origins and consequences of folk beliefs or knowledge structures, and others examine the sort of microcognitive processes and structures that are not represented in folk psychology. In this way, psychological theories that incorporate folk psychology may nevertheless produce insights that go beyond common sense or are even counterintuitive.

Finally, it is important to distinguish Use₁ of folk psychology from Use₂, a distinction that is expanded on in the next section.

Folk Psychology as a General Source in the Building of Overarching Theories in Psychology (Use₂)

In stark contrast to Use₁, to borrow folk beliefs, concepts, or approaches as part of scientific theory in terms of Use₂ does assume that such ideas are valid, plausible, or scientifically useful. The obvious related question (are we justified in so doing?) has already been touched on, and is discussed at length later in the book. For the moment, I outline a more straightforward empirical proposition—psychologists do in fact routinely make use of folk psychology in their theorizing (apart from the more restricted Use₁ outlined previously).

To begin with, most psychological theories contain certain fundamental assumptions of the sort that I have described in the previous chapter as inherently difficult to justify (e.g., that mental states or dispositions can cause behavior, and that knowledge structures are somehow stored in the mind). In addition, commonsense concepts and categories of all kinds abound in personality and social psychology and to a lesser extent in cognitive psychology—concepts such as *need, attitude, belief, emotion, drive, reward, punishment, attitude, intention, trait,* and so forth.

Empirical examinations of the similarity between lay theories and professional psychological theories confirm the existence of considerable overlap between the two spheres, partly in terms of Use$_2$ (for a review see Furnham, 1988). For example, substantial overlap has been found between lay conceptions and psychological theories concerning introversion–extroversion (Semin & Krahe, 1987), intelligence (Sternberg, Conway, Ketron, & Bernstein, 1981), delinquency (Furnham & Henderson, 1983), and depression (Rippere, 1977).

Let me take Sternberg et al.'s findings as an example of this research. Lay people and psychologists were first asked to list behaviors that were characteristic of "intelligence." The common characteristics were then rated by these two groups on Likert scales according to their importance in characterizing an idealized highly intelligent person, and the ratings were factor-analyzed. The results suggested that informal lay theories are similar to the psychologists' theories. Both conceptions, for example, included problem-solving ability (e.g., reasons logically and well), and verbal ability (e.g., is verbally fluent). However, the lay schema also included a factor that represented social competence (e.g., admits mistakes, is sensitive to other people's needs and desires, has a social conscience), a factor that was missing from the narrower more academically oriented schema produced by the experts' ratings. Interestingly enough, contemporary theories of intelligence have actually moved closer to the folk model, in that it has become fashionable to include a "social intelligence" factor into general definitions or theories of intelligence (e.g., Gardner, 1983).

There is considerable variability in the extent to which particular theories or domains within psychology exploit folk psychology for theory development in terms of Use$_2$. Cognitive theories have typically adopted some of the fundamental features of the folk psychology of mind. For example, with reference to Fig. 3.1, most cognitive theories maintain a folk-based distinction between cognitive dispositions and on-going processing, usually by distinguishing between long-term memory and working or short-term memory. Cognitive psychologists also frequently make distinctions between two basic kinds of online cognitive processing (see Holyoak & Spellman, 1993), some of which obviously have their genesis in folk psychology. For example, the folk notion that thinking and behavior vary in terms of controllability, has been picked up by Shiffrin and Schneider (1984) and used as the basis for an influential cognitive theory that distinguishes between controlled and automatic processing.

Of course, there remain important differences between scientific and folk models of cognition. For example, most scientific theories of cognition ignore the taxonomy of dispositions in folk psychology in terms of beliefs, attitudes, abilities, and the like, instead cutting up the dispositional cake in quite different ways. In Tulving's (1985) influential model, for example, the distinction is drawn among *episodic* and *semantic* long-term memory stores. Episodic memory refers to autobiographical memory and semantic memory refers to general knowledge about the world. Another popular distinction in cognitive psychology is between *declarative* and *procedural* memory. Declarative memory is concerned with facts and is essentially semantic in nature. Procedural memory is concerned with remembering skills or how to perform activities (e.g., riding a bike, driving a car).

Personality and social psychological theories, in contrast to standard cognitive models, have made greater use of the fine-grained elements in folk psychology. For example, personality theorists have appropriated the entire lexicon of folk traits in developing an overarching personality theory (more on this later). Social psychologists (unlike cognitive psychologists) have also made considerable use of some of the folk dispositional categories described in chapter 3 (see Fig. 3.1). For example, a large body of research and theorizing in social psychology has examined the function and nature of attitudes and their links to behavior (see McGuire, 1985, for a review). Another example is Ajzen's (1985; Ajzen & Madden, 1986) influential theory of planned behavior, which is clearly taken straight from folk psychology. In this model, the strength of an intention is the proximal cause that produces a behavior. The intention, in turn, is influenced by an individual's attitude to and beliefs about the behavior, beliefs about associated norms (is it right or wrong to perform this behavior?), and beliefs concerning the controllability of the behavior.

I conclude this section with a warning note that in practice it is sometimes not easy to tell if folk theory is being incorporated into scientific theories in terms of Use$_1$ or Use$_2$. I have much more to say concerning this point later in the chapter.

How Do Psychologists Appropriate Folk Psychology in Terms of Use$_2$?

There seem to be three major ways in which bits and pieces of folk psychology are incorporated into our master psychological theories (other than according to the Use$_1$ sense described previously). First, psychologists on occasion deliberately and explicitly exploit their own commonsense knowledge in designing theories. Second, folk ideas almost certainly implicitly inform the expert's theory-building process, in ways psychologists are blithely unaware of. Third, the methodologies used by psychologists sometimes automatically build folk theory into the overarching theory, a fact that is typically mentioned in passing or apparently goes unnoticed.

The first method (explicit use of folk psychology) is apparently benign, unless we were to believe that most commonsense thinking is false or implausible (a claim that has been made, but one I postpone dealing with until later).

The second procedure (unconscious or automatic use of folk psychology) is more worrisome, because it implies that folk psychology is being implicitly smuggled into our psychological theories in an uncontrolled way. The extent to which this occurs is bound to be variable, and may depend, in part, on how far the specialist knowledge base has developed in a particular field. Original theorizing in a given area has to be derived from some theoretical base, and if the specialist knowledge/theoretical base is minimal then informed common sense may be all one has. In addition, given the pervasive nature of our folk knowledge structures, the implicit acceptance of a set of commonsense fundamental assumptions (of the sort previously discussed), and our necessary reliance on a shared language (which carries cultural theoretical baggage), then a certain amount of leakage from our cultural/commonsense heritage into psychological theories is probably inevitable, and indeed necessary. A scientific theory that owed nothing to our folk cultural base, either in its content or the way it was expressed, would probably be unintelligible. Moreover, the fact that material from folk psychology is incorporated into scientific psychology (explicitly or implicitly) does not protect such concepts or ideas from critical scrutiny, argument, or empirical test—the fate of any theory of note in psychology. For example, the kind of sexist biases in Freudian theory (among others) have been effectively challenged over the last few decades by feminist academics (Riger, 1992).

This is not to say that psychological theories often do not willy-nilly incorporate values or ideas from folk psychology (as is clear from what I have been arguing), and these may escape critical scrutiny for a time. However, it is not plausible to view science as moving in perfect step with ideologies and ideas imported from the wider society. That this is often not the case is obvious to anyone with even a cursory understanding of the history of scientific development in any given field. To take one example, the development of Darwinian evolutionary theory was required to overcome deeply entrenched religious and scientific beliefs of the time. In psychology there are many examples of popular or successful theories that have gone against the conventional wisdom. Perhaps the most dramatic example is behaviorism (especially radical behaviorism), which dominated psychology for two decades and is four-square inconsistent with the mentalistic explanations of human behavior that were, and are, part and parcel of commonsense psychology.

The third process previously noted by which folk psychology is incorporated into psychology was termed the *methodological route.* This particular procedure is part of a more general problem in psychology where the two basic uses of folk psychology in psychological theorizing (Use₁ and Use₂) are, at times, run together in a confusing way, and with problematic results. I now turn to this important issue, first taking personality research as an example of how methodology can fatally blur the two domains. Other case studies in social psychology are also cited, including prototype emotion theory and attribution theory, to illustrate how the two categories are sometimes conflated at the theoretical level.

CONFOUNDING USE₁ AND USE₂ OF FOLK PSYCHOLOGY

Personality Research

There is compelling evidence from work in social psychology and social cognition that traits or personal dispositions are a central and pervasive component in folk psychology (see Newman & Uleman, 1989; Ross & Fletcher, 1985). Using a representative selection of such terms derived from the enormous lexicon in the English language, work by Norman (1963), Goldberg (1981), and more recently McCrae and his colleagues (McCrae & Costa, 1985) has shown that factor analyses of subjects' self-ratings reveal an underlying personality structure known as the

Big Five: extroversion, neuroticism, conscientiousness, agreeableness, and openness or intellect.

Now, personality theorists are invariably involved in the game of erecting master personality theories. And a typical part of this enterprise involves determining an appropriate taxonomy to order the multitude of personality dispositions—indeed, this is how the Big Five personality schema is interpreted by the psychologists just cited. Yet, clearly, what this research has actually revealed (accepting its validity for the moment) is one version of the outlines of our folk personality structure (at least as encoded in the English language). To accept the results as a reasonable base for a scientific personality theory is to implicitly vouchsafe the validity, plausibility, and usefulness of our commonsense thinking as it extends to this domain.

Given the enormity of this assumption, there has been remarkably little discussion in personality circles concerning the validity of this proposition, although personality theorists do occasionally indicate they are aware of the problem (e.g., McCrae & Costa, 1985).

However, other personality theorists seem less cognizant of the pitfalls of directly building a master theory from the materials of commonsense thought. For example, in Buss and Craik's (1983, 1984) act-frequency approach, naive raters are used to provide and rate the prototypicality of behavioral exemplars for a particular trait (e.g., dominance). The best items are then used as the set of measures for the trait in question. Clearly, such a procedure builds parts of folk psychology into the heart of the theory.

It should be understood here that Buss and Craik's personality theory does not represent such trait constructs as separate knowledge constructs within an overall model (a Use₁ procedure). Rather, the trait constructs essentially comprise the scientific personality theory; these personality constructs are not intended to represent lay usage, even though that is what they are. An analogous example would have been if I had interpreted the lay-perceived causes of relationship success, in the Close Relationships Belief Scale described earlier, as the basis for an expert theory concerning the *actual* causes of relationship success.

Emotion Theory

Over the last few decades there has been a burgeoning of interest in emotions in psychology (Strongman, 1987). And, not surprisingly given the developing cognitive zeitgeist over the same period, much of this work has adopted a cognitive perspective. Moreover, researchers have often been interested in the layperson's theories, knowledge structures, or concepts associated with different emotions.

One popular approach to analyzing such emotion knowledge structures has been derived from Rosch's (1978) work on concepts viewed as cognitive prototypes. According to Rosch, concepts are best viewed as consisting of a set of organized features that characterize a typical example of a particular object, event, or an emotion. They can be arranged along a vertical, hierarchical dimension and a horizontal dimension. For example, at the topmost level there is the general concept of emotion. At the middle-range level we have a list of what have sometimes been termed basic emotions, such as anger, fear, sadness, happiness, and disgust (to use a list recommended by Johnson-Laird & Oatley, 1989). At a lower level, such emotions will shade into more subtle emotions that will overlap strongly (e.g., sadness will include grief, poignancy, regretful, etc.). This approach is typically contrasted with the classical approach in which emotions are defined by defining features, so that different emotions can be precisely distinguished between.

The reader, by now, may be able to see the trouble brewing ahead—to wit, is a prototype or classical theory of concepts used by psychologists to simply give an account of the way that laypeople use emotion concepts (Use1), or does it represent a theory that scientists are supposed to use in the categorization of emotion concepts in their own overarching theories of emotion (Use2)?

A recent article by Russell (1991) shows the value of distinguishing between the two usages of folk psychology. Russell responded to criticisms of a prototype approach to emotions from a classical definitional perspective by citing research that suggests ordinary ways of thinking are consistent with a prototype, but not a classical approach to concepts. He admitted in closing that his arguments are defused if proponents of a classical approach to concepts are simply interested in conceptualizing emotions from an outside scientific perspective. But the problem, as he pointed out, is that it is not clear what the targets of a classically based theory are—the scientific concepts of the psychologist or those of the layperson.

Attribution Theory

Attribution theorists, from Heider (1958) to Kelley (1991), have stressed the difference between treating folk psychology as the subject matter of psychology (Use1), and exploiting commonsense concepts for use in our overarching theories (Use2). Yet, even in attribution theory these two aspects are sometimes mixed up. A good example of this is Shaver's (1985; Shaver & Drown, 1986) theory of the relations between causality, responsibility, and blame.

Shaver drew on much previous theoretical work and research to make the valid point that such concepts have often been methodologically and conceptually confounded in previous attribution work, with researchers often treating these concepts as interchangeable. Even minimal conceptual analysis of everyday examples indicates the folly of such a move. For example, an individual may have caused the bomb to go off in his car by switching on the ignition, but not be held responsible for it; or the person who supplied the bomb may be held responsible but not blamed for it because his own life was threatened; or a person who had knowledge of the car bomb may not have any causal role in the detonation, but be held partly responsible because he failed to contact the authorities.

Related attribution research backs up this analysis, in part, by showing that although causal judgments and attributional judgments with a strong evaluative/normative flavor (e.g., blame) are correlated, they are nevertheless not identical in lay theory (see Fletcher & Fincham, 1991; Shaver & Drown, 1986).

Based on such reasoning, Shaver and Drown suggested that responsibility and blame are made only after the occurrence of events that have negative consequences. Attributed responsibility is held to increase with the individual's (a) causal contribution to the effect, (b) awareness of the outcome, (c) intention to bring about the effect, (d) absence of external coercion, and (e) appreciation of the moral value of the action. Blame is finally a separate attribution made as a consequence of the offending person's justification or excuse.

Now, obviously, this theory is concerned with the task of describing how the layperson makes attributional judgments. But, Shaver and Drown (1986) then muddy the waters by treating the same account as a normative psychological theory that stands separate and above how people actually proceed. For example, they stated the following:

> It is not possible for a victim to be *objectively* blameworthy for the occurrence of a crime or an illness, unless the victim intentionally behaved in a manner to produce the suffering. This is not to say that victims are never blamed, by themselves or by others. Indeed, the manner in which blame is *inaccurately* applied by victims may prove valuable in understanding emotional adjustment. ... Researchers should also attend to whether the suffering was produced by a complex set of antecedants ... or by a single, specific action of the stimulus person. Only in the latter case would a self-attribution of causality be *veridical*, not withstanding the fact that almost any perceived control appears to be beneficial to the victims. (p. 710; italics added)

To derive a descriptive theory from research and conceptual analysis that is directly concerned with how laypeople think, should not then be used as a normative model to evaluate the correctness of commonsense judgments. To do so hopelessly confuses the two uses of folk psychology, and results in a muddle.

THE LEAKAGE OF SCIENTIFIC PSYCHOLOGICAL THEORIZING INTO FOLK PSYCHOLOGY

Up to now I have treated the overlap between scientific psychology and folk psychology as resulting from the incorporation (by psychologists) of folk psychology into professional psychological theories. But, of course, the flow may proceed in the opposite direction. This book is mainly concerned with the former causal relation, but this point merits some attention.

To begin with, there is good evidence that psychological theorizing has some impact on everyday thinking. Moscovici (1961/1976), for example has documented how psychoanalytic concepts, such as the unconscious and the superego, have infiltrated the everyday domain. In the United States, perhaps more than in any other country, it would not be surprising for psychology to exert an impact on the common culture. First, in the United States there is a ready acceptance of going to a psychologist, psychiatrist (one's shrink), or counselor. Second, there appears to be a mountain of pop-psychology available in the form of books, TV programs, radio shows, and so on. Third, the United States has a high rate of attendance at tertiary educational institutions (about 50%) where psychology is a popular subject, and psychology courses are also often taught at high schools. Accordingly, a good proportion of U.S. citizens have been exposed to at least a smattering of academic or clinically oriented psychology.

Perhaps for these reasons, concerned U.S. voices have been raised about the untoward effects of psychology on our ordinary ways of thinking and moral values. Wallach and Wallach (1983), for example, worry that what they see as the selfish and egocentric model of self that is contained in major psychological theories, will infect and damage our culture.

Such concerns about the invidious effects of scientific theories on our culture are hardly new. Darwinian theory, for example, has often been pilloried for its role in engendering and supporting godlessness, or the kind of greed, selfishness, competition, and conflict that are part of laissez-faire capitalism. For example, in a marvelous essay Gould (1991) examined what motivated William Jenning's Bryan (who was a notable progressive) to engage in his lengthy and ill-fated battle to outlaw the teaching of evolution, which ended up in the infamous Scopes "monkey" trial in 1925. He concluded that Bryan's central motivation was his conviction of the social evil of Darwinism. In Bryan's words, from his 1904 speech *The Prince of Peace*:

> The Darwinian theory represents man as reaching his present perfection by the operation of the law of hate—the merciless law by which the strong crowd out and kill the weak. If this is the law of our development then, if there is any logic that can bind the human mind, we shall turn backward toward the beast in proportion as we substitute (it for) the law of love. I prefer to believe that love rather than hate is the law of development. (see Bryan, 1909, pp. 268–269)

Bryan's convictions were in fact based on a set of popular misconceptions about Darwinian evolutionary theory, some of which have unfortunately been promulgated by scientists themselves (see Gould, 1991). However, it is important not to exaggerate the extent to which folk psychology is molded by any scientific discipline, including psychology. Folk psychology is a lumbering cultural animal, subject to many forces besides psychology, and is relatively slow to change.

In addition, there is bound to be a good deal of recycling, with folk psychology being incorporated into scientific psychology and then regurgitated as "expert" theories to a receptive public. For example, the kind of clinically based pyschologizing that is endemic in popular books and TV shows concerning close relationships seem remarkably derivative of commonsense beliefs about what produces relationship success (as a glance at Table 2.1 will show), almost invariably stressing good communication, working through conflict, establishing equitable relationships, and so forth.

When psychological theories are purveyed to the public that are starkly at odds with common sense, then folk psychology can be stubbornly resistant. A prime example of this sort of resilience is the influence that behaviorism has had on folk psychology. Behavioristic ideas held sway in academic psychology for about five decades, had a substantial spin-off effect on clinical psychology, and Skinner's own popularizations of his radical approach (with chilling titles like "Beyond Freedom and Dignity") were popular and read widely in the 1960s and 1970s. The net result of this propogandistic battering on the mentalism of folk psychology (much despised by Skinner) was apparently minimal. One reason for this is probably the ease with which one can conveniently (if mistakenly) reinterpret Skinnerian behaviorism to be consistent with folk psychology.

The term *reinforcer* has certainly made its way into the commonsense lexicon, but is almost always used as a synonym for *reward*, which it is not, or as a label for a pleasant emotion (as in "The reinforcer for watching the sunset is the happy feeling I obtain"), which is also wrong. Anyone who has taught psychology will know the difficulty in inculcating, into the heads of undergraduate students, the correct technical definitions of these terms. For the record, in Skinnerian Behaviorism, a positive reinforcer is any event that when added to the situation increases the probability of the prior behavior, and a negative reinforcer is any event that when taken away also increases the frequency of the behavior. Events that decrease the likelihood of a prior behavior (taken away or added) are known as punishers. Hence, if I increasingly watched the sunset as a reaction to my father telling me to stop wasting my time, then the positive reinforcer would be my father's admonitions; if I helped more round the house because my mother stopped nagging me, that would be a negative reinforcer; and, if I reduced my smoking because my wife offered me money, then that event would be a punisher. Hands up those who would have got one or more wrong.

CONCLUSION

In this chapter I have endeavored to outline how folk psychology and scientific psychology are in fact related. I argued that folk psychology is used in two distinct fashions in psychological theories: as one component of an overarching theory (Use1), or as a source of concepts or propositions that are used in the overarching theory itself (Use2). Examples were provided to show that psychologists sometimes confound these two categories at the methodological and theoretical levels, with dire consequences.

Later, I argue that philosophers have also slurred or ignored the Use1–Use2 distinction, with equally problematic results. For now, the stage is set for launching into the next phase of the book which further evaluates the arguments and controversies that have swirled around the question of how scientifically valid folk psychology is, both in terms of folk theory itself and in terms of the accuracy and rationality of lay social judgment.

Chapter 5
The Nature of Scientific Cognition:
A Realist Account

Having analyzed the nature and extent of the overlap between folk psychology and scientific psychology, I now turn to the even thornier question of what the relation should be between folk psychology and scientific psychology. In terms of the distinction drawn previously between Use₁ and Use₂, this second section of the book deals principally with Use₂—the use of folk psychology in the development of overarching psychological theories.

As previously noted, social psychologists, compared to cognitive scientists and philosophers, have adopted different and largely independent tacks in analyzing the scientific credibility of folk psychology. Within social psychology, a sustained and substantial research program over the last few decades has sought to empirically test the rationality and accuracy of common modes of social thought. In contrast, cognitive scientists and philosophers have concentrated on the scientific utility of folk psychology from a highly abstract and theoretical perspective that has focused on the usefulness of a handful of basic folk concepts such as attitudes and beliefs.

Whatever focus one adopts, judgments of the rational or scientific status of elements in folk psychology are inevitably normative judgments, based on comparisons between what ordinary folk do with some prescriptive scientific account. I have already proffered an account of what folk psychology consists of. In this section, I take up the other component of this comparison and outline what I take to be a scientific approach to psychology that consists of a contemporary version of scientific realism. As part of this account, I also analyze the merits and problems of two alternatives to scientific realism: traditional empiricism and relativism. Hopefully, this way of proceeding will make it clear why I hold to a version of scientific realism, and also perhaps help correct what I believe are some widespread misconceptions in psychology concerning scientific method.

In the 20th century up to the 1960s, mainstream psychology, along with philosophy of science, was, by and large, locked into a nonrelativist approach that assumed that there was a real world out there, and that scientific methods and reliance on systematic observation and experimentation were capable of giving us objective knowledge about that world.

This traditional approach (usually termed *positivism* or *empiricism*) was associated in psychology with a strict focus on behavior as the object of study, and with the acceptance of rigorous empirical research as the cornerstone of the scientific method. Some allowance was made for the use of cognitive variables, provided they were tied to observable reality by operational definitions (although Skinner fought a long but ultimately fruitless battle to eliminate mentalistic concepts).

However, over the last few decades this realist, empiricist account has suffered a sustained attack within psychology, with the principal alternative embracing a relativist approach. This clash between relativist and realist conceptions is an ancient battle, going back as far as Socrates. In the *Theaetetus* (at 171 AD), Socrates makes a sustained argument that a thoroughgoing relativism is self-refuting—an argument I expand on in due course. The latest incarnation of this debate in psychology has not blossomed in isolation, but is part of a zeitgeist in academic thinking and popular culture. Philosophers of science such as Feyerabend (1975) and Kuhn (1970) mounted successful and widely cited attacks on traditional empiricism, and proposed relativist alternatives. Indeed, empiricism and hypothetico-deductivism, at least in their pure forms, have largely been abandoned in contemporary philosophy of science. In addition, a plethora of influential academic movements with immaculate relativist credentials have recently emerged including what Bunge (1991, 1992) referred to as the new sociology of science, postmodernism in architecture and art (Silverman, 1990), and deconstructionism in literature and the philosophy of language (Norris, 1991). In psychology, relativism has emerged most strongly in the development of social constructionism (Gergen, 1985), discourse analysis (Potter & Wetherell, 1987), and feminist psychology (Riger, 1992), but relativist ideas can increasingly be found in many areas of psychology.

The usual strategy adopted by relativists is to first attack the validity of the traditional empiricist thesis, then expound the relativist alternative. However, these are not the only choices available. Indeed, over the last decade or so, philosophers of science have been busily constructing alternative realist conceptions of science that avoid the most problematic features of both empiricism and relativism. I present one version of such a postempiricist realist account in due course.

First, I outline some of the problems associated with the traditional empiricist approach. I next analyze the strengths and critical weaknesses of relativist approaches, and finally outline an alternative realist account that I believe is especially suitable for psychology. The central aim is to produce at least a sketch of an appropriate normative model of scientific inference, that can then be used to evaluate the scientific credibility of folk psychology.

PROBLEMS WITH TRADITIONAL EMPIRICISM

Traditional empiricist approaches in the social sciences are based on the following four assumptions:

1. A real world exists, independent of human existence, and the aims of the behavioral sciences are to explain, predict, and control human behavior.
2. Science is value free.
3. Theories and hypotheses are tested using objective and reliable methods to produce intersubjective observations.
4. Theories and variables are cashed out in terms of operational definitions.

This list, to some extent, represents a cardboard stereotype. Nevertheless, it describes with some accuracy the traditional empiricist position (for an example of a modern-day empiricist apologist see Kimble, 1989), and it is the stereotype remorselessly attacked by its relativist opponents.

As will be seen, the account I favor accepts the first assumption of the standard empiricist view (the aims of science, and the assumption of an external reality), but rejects, at least in part, the remaining three postulates. Relativism, however, challenges every component of an empiricist perspective, arguing that science is not value-free or politically neutral, and that data and observation are substantially influenced by the observer's theories; in short, that there is something radically mistaken in empiricism's tremendous reliance on data or observation as the guarantor of objectivity in theory assessment.

The Connection Between Theory and Data: The Empiricist Line

As I argue here, such relativist critiques have considerable force. In particular, there are serious problems with the key empiricist assumption that there exists a well-defined method or algorithm that decisively determines whether a theory is confirmed or disconfirmed by a set of data—problems I outline here.

Adherence to this particular maxim in psychology has probably been maintained by two ideas or practices. First, a commonly accepted general model of scientific inference in psychology is the hypothetico-deductive model, in which observational claims are deduced from theories then tested (Popper, 1959)—a model that places the entire burden of theory evaluation on the predictive accuracy of the theory. Second, psychology relies heavily on statistical significance tests to give straight yes or no answers as to whether the data support the hypothesis. In fact, it is apparent from the many trenchant criticisms of this standard approach that it has serious flaws (Cohen, 1990; Rosnow & Rosenthal, 1989). For example, it is hardly sensible that an effect at the $p = .049$ level is regarded as a significant finding, while an effect at the $p = .051$ level is treated as if the predicted finding was not obtained. To take another example, the fact that differences in sample size determine whether statistically significant effects are obtained creates difficulties in interpreting whether the results of such tests support a hypothesis or not.

However, even if the reforms pressed by Cohen (1990) and others were accepted, so that psychologists could more rationally assess the extent to which empirical findings were confirmatory of a given hypothesis, this would still not create the precise link between theory and data demanded by an empiricist approach. The reason is that there are a plethora of other factors to be considered when judging the credibility of an empirical test, apart from whether the data confirm the hypothesis. These factors include the strengths and weaknesses of the methodology used (e.g., experimental or correlational), the validity of the measures and the manipulations used, the appropriateness of the sample, the presence of artifactual variables, the presence of demand characteristics, the ecological validity of the research design, the initial plausibility of the theory, the plausibility of competing interpretations for the same data, and so the list could go on.

Hence, it is hardly surprising that disputes concerning the appropriate interpretation of research findings in relation to particular theories are endemic in psychology. For example, social psychology is full of controversies in which apparently disconfirming data have failed to convert the proponents of particular theories or hypotheses: Examples include the debate between self-perception theory and cognitive dissonance theory, the role of consensus information in social judgment, and the part played by introspection in social judgment (see Ross & Fletcher, 1985, for a discussion of these particular controversies).

Moreover, if we accept the sort of analyses carried out by philosophers of science of historically important episodes of scientific change (e.g., Kuhn, 1970; Laudan, 1984), then it is apparent that the slushy connection between theory and data is not idiosyncratic to psychology but is common to all sciences. A wonderful example is provided by Kelvin's arguments in the 1880s concerning the age of the earth (see Burchfield, 1975). Kelvin's calculations were based on the laws of thermodynamics, and were derived from three arguments concerning the cooling of the earth, the age of the sun, and the action of the tides. His preliminary estimates for the age of the earth, published in 1862, provided a figure of somewhere between 20 and 400 million years. However, over the subsequent years, he promulgated figures that were supposedly more accurate, and were increasingly lower. By 1897, his best estimate of the earth's age was 24 million, with an upper limit of around 40 million years.

Kelvin's estimates, as we now know, were widly astray (the earth is currently reckoned to be around 4.5 billion years old). But his work at the time provided an enormous challenge to Darwin's theory of evolution; namely, if the earth was as old as Kelvin claimed, there simply did not appear to be enough time for evolution to be accomplished along the lines suggested by Darwin's theory that postulated natural selection working on random genetic change.

How did Darwin and others respond to Kelvin's challenge? According to Burchfield's (1975) analysis, Darwin was painfully aware that his version of evolution was ruled out by Kelvin's estimates. However, after much intellectual wrestling, Darwin was disposed to recommend a wait-and-see attitude while continuing to push his own theory. Others, such as Huxley and Wallace (the co-discoverer of Evolution), altered Darwin's theory to allow for natural catastrophes or rapid climatic changes to accelerate the pace of evolution that would be more usual in stable periods. However, as Kelvin's estimates of the earth's age became ever lower, geologists and others adopted a more confrontational perspective and began questioning Kelvin's original analyses. As was often argued, if the evidence from physics and geology conflict, why should geology necessarily submit?

The decisive blow to Kelvin's estimates did not come until 1906, when Ernest Rutherford (who happens to be the University of Canterbury's most famous student) realized that the discovery of radiation (an internal source of heat) enormously increased the possible age of the earth and the solar system.

My general point, however, is not that scientists were irrational prior to 1906. In retrospect, the way in which Kelvin's arguments were dealt with by Darwin and his followers seem rational and remarkably percipient. Nor am I claiming that empirical findings do not play a critical role in major theoretical shifts, such as the shift from Newtonian mechanics to relativity theory or the shift from behavioral to cognitive paradigms. Rather, my general claim is that the empirical evidence does not appear to be used in the straightforward way implied by empiricist doctrine. In psychology, as in the rest of science, even when the validity of an inconsistent finding is granted, a common response is to modify rather than to abandon the extant theory, or even to ignore the inconsistent data. Science is inherently conservative with respect to theory change, and for good reason given that scientists are so often confronted with competing theories that carry evidential support.

The core of the argument can be summed up in the aphorism that *theory is underdetermined by data*. Hence, there is no data-based algorithm that unequivocally dictates theory selection. Rather, theory evaluation within a scientific community is typically a messy affair often involving inconsistent and contradictory evidence.

Operational Definitions and What's Wrong With Them

Another facet of traditional empiricism's emphasis on observational data is the way in which cognitive attributions are rendered acceptable by tying them to observable behavior via operational definitions. To operationally define a cognitive attribution is to exhaustively detail the meaning of the concept in terms of the observable behavior. The long recognized problem with this strategy is that seemingly vacuous explanations are then produced. In Kimble's (1989) words:

> If someone says that a man has hallucinations, withdraws from society, lives in his own world, has extremely unusual associations, and reacts without emotion to imaginary catastrophes because he is a schizophrenic, it is important to understand that the word because has been misused. The symptomatology defines (diagnoses) schizophrenia. The symptoms and the cause are identical. The "explanation" is circular and not an explanation at all. (p. 495)

Positivists, like Kimble, gladly accept such a consequence arguing that cognitive attributions are merely handy concepts rather than representative of real entities or causal structures. But, if cognitive attributions are simply proxies for descriptions of the environment and/or behavior, which are observable and thus carry the weight of any explanation, then why bother to refer to intervening variables in the first place (Greenwood, 1992)? Such attributions would seem to offer nothing in terms of the traditional aims of psychology that Kimble (1989) approvingly cited: explanation, prediction, and control.

THE RELATIVIST SOLUTION AND ITS ACHILLES' HEEL

The radical relativist solution to the sort of problems that traditional empiricism suffers from is a wholesale repudiation of all that empiricism stands for, including its aims, values, and methods. Of course, there are differences among relativist approaches, but here I focus on four common themes among three popular relativist approaches in psychology today: social constructionism, discourse analysis, and postmodern versions of radical feminism.

First, relativist approaches stress the equivalence of scientific and lay accounts or theories of human behavior. Different theories are regarded as alternative ways of construing the world, to be described or analyzed rather than evaluated in terms of their predictive power, explanatory value, or truth value. Thus, in their postmodern analysis of gender, Hare-Mustin and Marecek (1988) argued that because "the real nature of male and female cannot be determined" we should "focus our attention on representations of gender, rather than on gender itself" (p. 458), and analyze the way in which such representations organize and influence scientific theories and therapeutic practice. In a similar vein, discourse analysis treats scientific theories and folk accounts alike as texts to be analyzed and deconstructed, rather than evaluated in terms of their truth value (Potter & Wetherell, 1987).

Second, the focus of psychology is held to be at the social level—the individual's behavior and cognition are viewed as products of the wider collective, and mainstream psychology is charged with being overly individualistic (Gergen, 1985, 1989). Exactly the same analysis is provided for scientific theories and approaches. Thus, some feminist analyses argue that western empiricist science, with its values of objectivity, truth, and control is derivative of androcentric values and norms: Science is, thus, a distinctly male institution (see Riger, 1992).

Third, such approaches emphasize the role of language, both as the object of study and as the central instrument by which social life is represented and constructed.

Fourth, empiricist aims such as truth, control, or explanation are dropped. In their place, theories are evaluated in political terms, according to their political and social ramifications. In Gergen's (1985) social constructionism, for example, theories are acceptable to the extent that they challenge the social order, or enrich and empower people's lives. Postmodernist versions of feminist psychology strike a similar theme: Theories should principally challenge the prevailing dominant and repressive male scientific ideologies and empower women (Riger, 1992).

I focus here on what I believe is the fatal Achilles' heel of all such relativist positions; namely, by discarding the criteria or aims concerned with truth or objectivity and adopting a full-blown constructionism, such theories become entangled in a fatal web of internal contradictions. As already noted, this general criticism of relativism is not new, first being enunciated by Socrates (see Siegel, 1987, for an excellent book-length analysis and account of the problems with relativism).

For example, how does one evaluate a relativist thesis, such as Gergen's version of social constructionism? We cannot do so on the basis of criteria such as its predictive or explanatory power, or on any judgment concerning its truth value, because that is to commit ourselves a priori to its rejection given that the theory itself is built on the dismissal of such values and concepts.

We also cannot evaluate social constructionism in terms of its aims, because it is not clear how this is possible without considering their associated truth values. If assessing whether theories do actually challenge the social order or enrich people's lives is not possible, or is simply an outcome of whichever theory is arbitrarily adopted, then such aims become vacuous.

A problem also arises with how to interpret the welter of empirical claims (from the mundane to the pivotal) that underpin the arguments of those expounding relativist positions. To take a few examples from the hundreds available, Gergen (1985) stated that "The degree to which a given form of understanding prevails or is sustained across time is not fundamentally dependent on the empirical validity of the perspective in question, but on the vicissitudes of social processes" (p. 268), and that "The mounting criticism of the positivist-empiricist conception of knowledge has severely damaged the traditional view that scientific theory serves to reflect or map reality" (p. 266), and that "its proponents are legion" (p. 266). In the course of their article expounding a (highly relativist) postmodernist version of feminism, Hare-Mustin and Marecek (1988) stated that "males have had privileged access to education and thus have had higher rates of literacy" (p. 455), that "Outgroups such as women are viewed as more homogenous than dominant groups" (p. 459), and that "postmodernism makes us aware of connections among meaning, power, and language" (p. 461).

On the face of it, it seems difficult if not impossible to sensibly interpret such claims, and in turn to evaluate the wider theses, without taking seriously the issue of whether such claims are true or false. But of course, to do so undercuts the relativist thesis itself.

One possible rejoinder to this line of argument is that Gergen and other relativists do not present their accounts as true in the ordinary sense of the word; rather, they may be simply inviting us to take a given perspective, much as we might be invited to sample a new flavor of ice cream. As Gergen (1985) himself said, the success of theoretical accounts "depends primarily on the analyst's capacity to invite, compel, stimulate, or delight the audience, and not on criteria of veracity" (p. 272). To take a leaf from discourse analysis, empirical claims might therefore be interpreted purely as rhetorical devices intended to persuade or convince the reader.

To take a quote from Gergen (1989) again:

truth and objectivity may largely be viewed as rhetorical devices. They are for example useful in rendering praise or allocating blame. We reward a child for "telling the truth" not because he has accurately reported on the state of his sensory neurons, but because his report accords with our adult conventions. When we prize the medical specialist who discovers a fatal illness just in time for remedy, it is not because she has seen the body for what it is. Rather, she has carried out a series of practices (along with socially agreeable modes of indexing) that eventuate in what we conventionally call "the prolonging of life." (p. 473)

Now, one standard rebuttal to such arguments is that reality is simply not as malleable as suggested in relativist positions: that, for example, whether penicillin cures bacterial infections is a matter of fact, regardless of how related events are imbedded in social practices. But the general argument I am presenting is more lethal to relativism than simply the observation that it represents a bizarre doctrine; to wit, that relativist arguments concerning the rhetorical functions of empirical or truth claims again face the spectre of self-contradiction. For example, in arguing that "truth" and "objectivity" function as rhetorical devices, Gergen made various claims about the most appropriate or plausible way of describing the world—for example, that the grounds on which we reward children are x and not y. Such empirical claims cannot be evaluated, nor even rendered intelligible, without considering their associated truth values.

In summary, social constructionist and relativist arguments regularly make use of the same criteria of veracity, including empirical claims, that are simultaneously discarded as relics of a positivist tradition. However, in sawing off the branch that holds up the values of rationality, truth, and belief in a world that is (partly at least) independent of human cognition, relativists apparently fail to realize that they are perched on the same part of the branch they are busily attempting to sever. A strong relativism is self-refuting, and is, hence, not tenable.

Finally, it seems to me that relativism provides a chilling spectre of how science should proceed; to wit: Science should be disinterested in truth and is inevitably the handmaiden for a wider political order. In fact, we have several real-world examples of such a prescription including Nazi Germany and the USSR. In the USSR, for example, biological and agricultural science was dominated for over three decades, up to the 1960s, by Lysenko who developed a radical form of Lamarkian theory against Mendelian gene theory. Scientists who upheld Mendelian theory were held to be politically incorrect and labeled as racist, pro-Western, and anti-Marxist. Through the political power Lysenko attained, scientists who refused to publicly subscribe to his views were also fired and jailed in their hundreds (Medvedev, 1969).

Given that "science" in these totalitarian political systems was located within justificatory normative frameworks, the challenge for relativists is to say why such arrangements are suspect or wrong. The reason this represents such a daunting project is that relativism has dispensed with the very notion of correctness or cognitive superiority. Any theory with its associated set of societal values is as good as another. When truth goes out the window and science is seen as purely a political institution, then might presumably becomes right.

It is important to note that this general argument against relativist positions in psychology does not necessarily invalidate all the seminal ideas that have been developed in relativist critiques of traditional empiricism. For example, even if a thoroughgoing relativism is successfully refuted it could still be posited that science is a socially constituted construction, that science is not value free, and, as already argued, that there is a much looser connection between data and theory confirmation (or disconfirmation) than assumed in empiricist doctrine.

However, I argue that acceptance of such propositions is not necessarily inimical to a realist account. For example, consideration of societal influences on our theories and methods can raise important questions, remove unconscious sources of bias, and lead to more powerful or plausible theories. Moreover, the fact that psychological theories and debates are influenced by societal beliefs, does not mean that they are not also settled according to rules, norms, and aims that are essentially rational or epistemic in character (see Bunge, 1992). Indeed, it is this rational structure, rejected in the relativist scheme of things and oversimplified in the empiricist conception, that I now outline in the context of a realist approach to psychological science. In so doing, I hope to show how the problems attendant on the traditional empiricist account can be avoided without retreating to a strong relativist position.

AN ALTERNATIVE ACCOUNT: SCIENTIFIC REALISM

I first make a few general points concerning this account. The particular model I explicate here is an amalgam of ideas drawn from a variety of sources. However, this model is presented in a novel way and is slanted toward psychology. Hence, it has some original features. (For some psychological treatments of realist approaches see Fletcher, in press; Greenwood, 1989; Howard, 1985; Manicas & Secord, 1983. For more philosophically oriented accounts see Bhaskar, 1978; Hooker, 1987; McMullin, 1984.)

The four major headings (Aims, Values, Rules, and Theories; see Fig. 5.1) are intended to apply to psychology generally. In addition, there is clearly some overlap among the four categories. This facet is most apparent comparing the Values with the Aims, both of which refer to similar concepts (prediction, explanation, etc.).

The Theories category simply applies to the actual psychological theories themselves. The Aims in the model are the standard aims of psychology that could be found in any introductory textbook of psychology. The Epistemic Values section comprises the criteria to be used in evaluating and comparing theories. The multiplicity of such criteria means that predictive accuracy is not the sole criterion for theory choice; hence, a crude empiricism is avoided, along with the problems already outlined that are produced when the entire burden of theory evaluation falls on empirical testing. However, this version of scientific realism accepts that theory evaluations will always consist of judgment calls that are prone to error.

In the remaining sections, I first discuss truth as a scientific aim in detail. This is an important and controversial topic and is central to understanding what makes

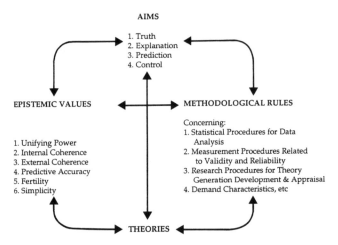

FIG. 5.1.   A realist version of scientific rationality.

this realist approach tick. Next, the Epistemic Values and Methodological Rules are described, and the connections among the four components discussed. Finally, the question is posed as to whether the present realist model can avoid collapsing into full-blown relativism.

Truth as a Scientific Aim

According to standard realist accounts, scientific theories postulate theoretical entities or causal structures to explain phenomena. Some of these theoretical entities are unobserved (e.g., cognitive mechanisms in psychology or subatomic particles in physics). It is a central contention of this version of scientific realism that such theories are intended to adequately refer to and represent the world, some aspects of which are independent of human cognition. Hence, science aims to construct true theories.

However, it is important to note that in this account the relation between the "theory" and the "world" is seldom like a simple mirror image or picture. Rather, it is proposed that theories represent or map onto the world in a relatively abstract fashion (cf. Hooker, 1987). Cognitive theories, for example, represent the neuro-physiological machinery in terms of information flow. Cognitive models may refer to real structures and brain events, but in an abstract or indirect fashion that represent certain functional and organizational features inhering in neurophysio-logical structures (a theory of mind already described known as functionalism; Fodor, 1991).

The standard argument for a functionalist account of the mind is in terms of an analogy with the same computer program running on two computers with different hardware. The computer program can be likened to a theory specifying what is happening inside the computer in terms of information storage, retrieval, and computation. Likewise, the same information-processing software could be instantiated in two brains with different hardware (i.e., neurophysiological structures and processes). Of course, just as computer programs are constrained to some extent by the hardware so cognitive theories will need to be consistent with our knowledge of neurophysiological processes and structures.

It should be noted that although science aims at developing true theories, it is an essential element of modern scientific thinking that one remains skeptical of one's truth claims. To reiterate an earlier theme, it is important to rebut the notion (often assumed in the media) that science is in the business of offering iron-clad evidence—presumably such a view is the well-spring for that egregious phrase "scientific proof." Rather, the drive toward truth is better conceptualized as a guiding ideal or idealized horizon (McMullin, 1983), which can be thought of as a highly valued, although unobtainable, goal of scientific enquiry.

To illustrate this point, imagine asking a psychologist to state whether any modern psychological theory is true or false. Instead of an unequivocal judgment backed up by indisputable proof, one will almost certainly receive a reply couched in terms that suggest doubt and uncertainty. Even the most favored theory will be described as having problems, as incomplete, and as offering the best theoretical interpretation of the extant research evidence. Perhaps none of this is surprising given the complexity of the subject matter being modeled. More generally, however, many psychologists are, I think, uncomfortable with hard and fast truth claims because such claims run counter to important scientific norms that include maintaining a skeptical attitude and remaining open to alternative theoretical interpretations.

In summary, the pivotal thesis I am concerned with establishing here is that in this brand of realism theories are intended to model or represent the structural and causal properties of the world, even when that world is not directly observable, such as is the case with subatomic particles or cognitive states and processes. This aim decisively divorces scientific realism from the traditional empiricist account that interprets cognitive structures, via operational definitions, as either empirically empty formal accounts or simply as conceptual stand-ins for observable reality.

Scientific realism avoids the problem of a vicious circularity, already described, that occurs with the use of operational definitions within a traditional empiricist framework. Of course, it is eminently acceptable, even a logical necessity, that any attempt to measure a cognitive construct will involve an observable criterion; but such a criterion can be viewed as one imperfect measure of a cognitive construct rather than as an exhaustive theoretical definition. Consider, for example, the use of reaction times, self-report scales, or incidental recall tasks in psychology. The related subject behaviors can be, and often are, viewed as imperfect measures of theoretical constructs. In turn, such constructs would be defined in terms of a general model or construct that would typically include references to whole classes of cognitive or affective constructs, judgments, and behaviors.

Moreover, contra positivism, cognitive, affective, or personality/trait constructs are often regarded in contemporary psychology as referring to entities or systems that play a bona fide causal role in generating cognition or behavior, although there remains considerable controversy in psychology over this issue with respect to personality dispositions (Fletcher, 1993). In this regard, it is easy to misconceive psychology as being more empiricist than it is, because terms like *operational definitions* and *operationalization* are still bandied around both in textbooks and research reports. However, such terms are often misleadingly used in the innocuous sense already described; namely, to refer to observable measures of an underlying construct rather than as exhaustive theoretical definitions.

MacCorquodale and Meehl's (1948) well-known distinction is between intervening variables that are operationally defined, and hypothetical constructs that carry surplus theoretical meaning and cannot be reduced to observational criteria. According to this usage, cognitive and affective constructs in contemporary psychology would appear to be almost wholly hypothetical constructs. The reader should be warned, however. The term *intervening variable* is sometimes wrongly used in the psychological literature to refer to all cognitive or internal variables (including hypothetical constructs).

Epistemic Values

The list of epistemic values used in evaluating the worth of particular theories are shown in Fig. 5.1 (see Howard, 1985). A theory that manages to integrate and explain hitherto disparate items of knowledge possesses the valuable property of unifying power. A theory whose content is logically consistent has internal coherence, while a theory that is consistent with other entrenched or accepted theoretical knowledge has the virtue of external coherence. The value of predictive accuracy is satisfied by a theory whose test predictions square adequately with the data. As for fertility, this refers to the ability of a theory to stimulate further fruitful lines of research or generate novel and powerful extensions to our knowledge base. Finally, the notion of simplicity has proved difficult to formulate; nevertheless, scientists are frequently attracted by theoretical elegance rather than cumbersome complexity.

Methodological Rules

The Methodological Rules section is intended to represent the cognitive accompaniment to professional research and statistical procedures. These consist of rules of thumb or principles to be considered in the design of research, the proper analysis and interpretation of data, and so forth: rules that are taught to students in methodology and statistics classes. It seems to me (and others) that it is the special character of the methodological issues confronted by psychologists that most decisively distinguishes psychology (and the social sciences generally) from the physical sciences, these issues being rooted in the special nature of human beings (Howard, 1985). For example, it is because human beings are self-conscious, language-using, information-processing animals that the problem of demand characteristics is such a thorny research issue in psychology, but not in physics. Communicating one's hypotheses to inanimate matter will not alter its behavior one whit. Doing the same with human beings is quite likely to do so—hence, the common need for deception in psychological research with its accompanying ethical problems.

Connections Among the Four Categories

The double-headed arrows in this model indicate that the elements in this system are interactive, so that every component can influence any other component. This approach can be contrasted with the more usual hierarchical approach, in which aims and methodological rules determine theories but not the other way around. Laudan (1984) gave examples from the natural sciences to support his view that causal influences among these categories flow in all directions.

Such an interactive account also appears to fit psychology well. Consider, for example, the influence that psychological theories exert on methodological rules in psychology. Because psychological theories in cognitive and social psychology often deal with deep-level theoretical constructs, psychologists in these domains are very concerned with issues of construct validity, and many of the innovative statistical and methodological developments have arisen in response to such concerns (e.g., causal modeling). In addition, social psychological theories are built on the assumption that human beings actively process and act upon information— hence the researcher's concern that subjects will ascertain and deliberately comply with the researcher's hypothesis (the problem of demand characteristics). In contrast, radical behaviorism is less concerned with issues of construct validity because psychological variables are construed in terms of observable molar behaviors or physical events (rather than deep-structural theoretical constructs). Moreover, the issue of demand characteristics is not usually singled out by radical behaviorists as a special problem because they hold that the causes of human behavior should be viewed as located outside the organism; hence, the human organism is viewed as a responder to environmental events, not as an active information processor.

However, influence may also flow in the opposite direction to that just described, with methodological rules affecting psychological theories. Gigerenzer (1991) argued, for example, that statistical theories and approaches have influenced the theories of mind developed in psychology. One example from social psychology is the way Kelley (1967) developed his influential model of attributional processes using the statistical procedure of analysis of variance as his theoretical base for how the layperson computes causal inferences.

Finally, an important point here is that the links in the model are loose and multifaceted and do not seem to operate according to some precise algorithm. Laudan (1984) traced this looseness of fit to his claim that scientific change in the physical sciences tends to occur in a much more piecemeal fashion than implied in Kuhn's (1962) influential analysis. In Kuhn's account, scientific change is portrayed in terms of sweeping paradigm changes that interrupt the more usual pattern of normal science that runs within set theoretical paradigms.

Interestingly, Laudan's analysis again applies well to psychology. Sweeping theoretical changes have of course occurred in psychology, with the shift from a behaviorist to a cognitive perspective sometimes cited as the classic example. But this shift has occurred in a piecemeal fashion. For example, social psychology has always been cognitive in its orientation even in the behaviorist heyday, and decades prior to the cognitive revolution influential neobehaviorist theories were advanced that shared aspects of both cognitive and behavioral models of human behavior (e.g., Tolman's, 1932, approach, which he termed *purposive behaviorism*).

Kuhn (1962) characterized normal science as free of basic theoretical dispute and devoted toward solving anomalies and puzzles within an accepted theoretical paradigm. This certainly sounds like a reasonable enough description of much research in psychology. However, against a Kuhnian analysis, in psychology this more detailed work has often operated against a backdrop of fervent dispute concerning more general theoretical issues and questions.

The cognitive "revolution" may have won out in psychology, but has been replaced by such bedrock battles in cognitive psychology as the merits of a parallel distributed processing model versus the standard computational account (Fodor & Pylyshyn, 1988). Fundamental disputes in social psychology are also alive and well concerning the appropriate kind of methodological and statistical principles (Rosnow & Rosenthal, 1989), and the proper role of the "social" in social psychology (Harré, 1989). Indeed, perhaps influenced by a Kuhnian approach, critics have been describing the state of affairs in mainstream social psychology as being at crisis point at regular intervals over the last three decades—a theoretical paroxysm that has assumed a permanent existence!

One popular notion is that psychology is considerably more disputatious at a basic theoretical level than the natural sciences, a proposition sometimes conjoined with an expressed yearning for psychology to develop the unity evinced by the natural sciences (e.g., Staats, 1991). However, my own reading and understanding of disciplines such as physics, astronomy, and palaeontology leads me to think that the natural sciences are just as given to fundamental and fractious argument as is psychology. To take just one apposite example from physics (often considered the paradigm of sciences), subatomic nuclear physics has been rent for decades with a debate concerning a relativist versus realist interpretation of subatomic reality. The Copenhagen interpretation of quantum mechanics developed in the 1930s offers an extreme relativist view that subatomic events are dependent on human observation, while Einstein along with more recent theorists have championed a realist interpretation (see Horgan, 1992; Jabs, 1992).

Now of course, disputes are often resolved and consensus is commonly forged. The point I am making is rather that dispute and disagreement, from the nit-picking to the grandiose, are permanent features of psychology, or any other science, that exist alongside the more mundane problem solving that occurs within theoretical and methodological paradigms.

Summary

The scientific realist approach outlined owes much to its empiricist forebears. However, I argued that it is critically distinct from a traditional empiricist approach in that less reliance is placed on data or observation. Hence, in the current approach, operational definitions are dispensed with and the predictive validity of a theory constitutes but one criterion (albeit a central one) among several used in theory evaluation. Moreover, it is clear that this model embraces a limited brand of relativism, in that psychologists can, and do, disagree about the relative importance of particular values or beliefs in evaluating theories. In addition, I previously strenuously argued (see chapter 2) against foundationalism, and in this chapter posited a thoroughgoing skepticism as a central pivot of scientific thinking. Accordingly, no part of the scientific realist model advanced here should be considered as, in principle, immune to revision. These admissions could be regarded as inexorably leading back to a full-blown relativism, a suggestion I now turn to.

Relativism: Lost But Regained?

The conclusion that the present version of realism lands up back in a thoroughgoing relativism is forestalled on several counts. First, the fact that no part of the model is immune to revision does not mean that all components are equally susceptible to revision. For example, this model will embrace certain critical, fundamental beliefs that are, as a matter of contingent fact, difficult to dispose of without also jettisoning the possibility of understanding the world in an intelligible fashion (Fletcher, 1984). As I argued in chapter 2, an extreme skeptic could argue that the laws of logic, the existence of an external world, or the durability of causal processes, are difficult if not impossible to justify in some absolute sense. Indeed, I would agree. However, jettisoning any one of these beliefs is in practice difficult to maintain in everyday life without descending into either madness or silence.

Second, it can plausibly be argued that observational descriptions (data) are typically products of our perceptual systems and are accordingly more directly connected to the external world than are inferential judgments derived from reasoning or other higher order cognitive processes, such as evaluations of a theory (see Clark & Paivio, 1989; Fodor, 1983; Gilman, 1992). Hence, although psychologists regularly disagree concerning which theory best explains a particular set of research results they are usually in agreement concerning descriptions of those data, especially where such descriptions are expressed in simple, commonsense observational terms (e.g., rats pressing bars, time taken to press a computer key, and circling numbers on Likert scales). This point is consistent with the fact that disputes in psychology are hardly ever concerned with basic-level descriptions of data, but rather focus on the appropriate theory with which to interpret the data or on technical points such as design or data analytic issues.

These arguments also bear on the often raised relativist thesis that adherents of different theoretical paradigms live in conceptually sealed theoretical worlds, rendering communication problematic even at the level of crude data—a thesis termed the *incommensurability of theories* by Kuhn (1962). Data, so the argument goes, are impregnated with theory and so data descriptions in one theory have no logical equivalent in the context of a competing theory.

Of course, it would be foolish to deny that theories substantially influence the sort of data collected, as indeed I have previously argued. Clearly, commitments to theoretical paradigms help determine the content and design of the research, the kind of data collected, and the higher order descriptions of those data (e.g., categorizing data as "reinforcers" or "subjects' attitudes"). However, as previously pointed out, scientists will generally share a common understanding of what the data mean at a basic descriptive level. It may certainly be hard for scientists to imaginatively think their way into competing theoretical approaches, and scientists holding radically different theories do tend to talk past one another. But although these tasks are difficult they are not in principle impossible.

CONCLUSION

Individual psychologists will of course fail to match up to the kind of high falutin' values presented here, and will occasionally behave irrationally, hang onto their favorite theory in spite of the evidence, and sometimes even fabricate data or tell lies. But such falls from grace are not evidence that the model is inadequate, but rather the opposite, indicating the way in which such a set of values and goals might help scientists to tread the rational high road and to recognize those occasions when others fail to do so.

It is precisely because such a system of scientific inference is an evolving, socially constructed product, with links to the wider society, that the postmodernists' proposal that science be regarded as simply another political institution with cast-iron links to the wider society is disturbing. It is because the sort of model being promoted here is consistent with, and supportive of, the traditions and values of an open society, in which debate and the freedom to disagree are basic and the primary duties of science are epistemic not political, that the postmodern alternative presents such a chilling spectre. However, I have tried to show that the choice is not simply between relativism and a traditional empiricism. Postempiricist versions of realism are available that fit comfortably within modern-day psychology, but that avoid the pitfalls of both empiricism and relativism.

Having described, at least roughly, an account of science from an epistemic perspective I am now in a position to compare the layperson to this picture. I proceed by taking each component in turn (Aims, Epistemic Values, Methodological Rules, and Theories) and asking the question: Is this how the layperson thinks about social phenomena? To anticipate my conclusions, it is argued that the world of commonsense cognition is continuous with and overlaps the science of psychology in complex ways that depend on the component of rationality one considers. Generally, however, it will turn out that folk psychology is surprisingly scientific.

Chapter 6
The Scientific Status of Folk Psychology 1: Lay Aims, Values, and Rules

As noted in the introduction, the idea that human lay social cognition was rational or scientific was in tatters by the mid-1980s. A good deal of research on errors and biases documented an extraordinary range of invidious social judgment biases, including the underutilization of base rates, the fundamental attribution error, the confirmation bias, belief perseverance, and overconfidence in social judgment. Laypeople came to be seen as lazy thinkers, as incompetent statisticians, and as hopelessly biased by their frequently wrong-headed social theories (e.g., Fiske & Taylor, 1984; Nisbett & Ross, 1980). Rather than being like scientists, laypeople came to be seen as more akin to *cognitive misers*, driven by pragmatic aims, and with a poor understanding of scientific rules of inference.

More recent research, however, has suggested that that such a bleak view of human rationality is, at best, a half truth. In this chapter I use the general model of scientific cognition previously proposed as a tool for organizing an analysis and review of the psychological research and theoretical argument that bears on the central question: How scientific is lay (social) cognition? I begin with the layperson's aims, then examine lay use of epistemic values, and finally move to a discussion of the ordinary person's understanding of methodological or inference rules.

HOW SCIENTIFIC ARE THE AIMS OF THE LAYPERSON?

It is almost a truism that goals such as truth, prediction, control, and understanding, are fundamental aims for all forms of life. The ability to survive and procreate, for example, is founded on an animal's success in predicting and exercising control over the environment, and its ability to accurately represent the important features of that environment.

Not surprisingly, therefore, the importance of such goals is accepted by many psychologists. Most social cognitive models or theories have such goals explicitly or implicitly built in, and there is a wealth of research that illustrates or demonstrates the power of such goals in the generation of social judgments and behavior. However, a small band of psychologists have argued that lay goals are fundamentally different to those of the scientist, and have raised two principal arguments in support of such a view.

The first argument posits that people are more interested in practical concerns, such as making money or maintaining personal relationships, than building explanatory models (Friedrich, 1993; Swann, 1984; White, 1984). On this account, people are viewed as pragmatists rather than as scientists. The second challenge to the lay scientist model argues that epistemic aims typically play second fiddle to the aim of retaining a flattering and positive self-concept (Greenwald, 1980; Taylor & Brown, 1988). According to this view, people are best viewed as Pollyannas, rather than as scientists. I consider each argument in turn.

Laypeople as Pragmatists

First, although it is obvious that laypeople are pragmatists in the sense that they are often interested in attaining practical goals, there is good evidence of individual differences in the extent to which people are interested in goals such as prediction, control, and explanation in everyday life. Reliable self-report scales have been developed by psychologists that measure such constructs as the desire for control (Burger & Cooper, 1979), the need for cognition (Cacioppo & Petty, 1982), and attributional complexity (Fletcher, Danilovics, Fernandez, Peterson, & Reeder, 1986). These three scales contain items such as: "I prefer a job where I have a lot of control over what I do and when I do it," "Thinking is not my idea of fun," and "I am not really curious about human behavior."

These three scales (desire for control, need for cognition, and attributional complexity) are in fact moderately positively correlated at around the .4 level (see Fletcher et al., 1986; Thompson, Chaiken, & Hazlewood, 1993). There is also good evidence that these constructs are not related to IQ or academic performance, but that they are related to how well various cognitive activities are performed. That is, people's self-reports of their interest in goals such as control and explanation, are not merely self-flattering opinions that bear no relation to everyday thinking and behavior. More on this topic later. For the moment, the point I wish to make is that there is good evidence that people vary in terms of how motivated they are in pursuing scientific-like aims in relation to human behavior. In a nutshell, some people seem to be more like prototypical scientists than others, at least in terms of their goals.

Second, the view that explanatory activity is typically motivated by practical goals, including prediction and control, is not antithetical to a lay scientist model. Indeed, the standard scientific realist approach is based on the proposition that an understanding of underlying causal processes and structures will be helpful or even indispensable in predicting and controlling related events. Moreover, it seems likely that this realist assumption is embedded in commonsense thinking. Casual observation suggests that people often believe that problems such as unemployment, violent behavior, or relationship problems, will be dealt with more effectively if we understand their causes. These anecdotal impressions are buttressed by the one study that, to my knowledge, has directly addressed this question. Forsterling and Rudolph (1988) reported that people who are guided by attributions perceived as lacking veridicality are judged by others as less likely to achieve long-term success in both achievement and social situations. For example, students who failed an exam and wrongly concluded that they were dumb, or passed an exam and wrongly concluded that they were bright, were judged by raters as less likely to be successful in the future, compared to students who made these same attributions but based on solid evidential grounds.

The view that explanations are often motivated by the need for control or prediction is supported by the body of research that suggests attributional activity is particularly motivated by unexpected events or failure to attain goals (for a review see Weiner, 1985). When people fail something, or face an unexpected event they ask why, presumably in an attempt to gain control over future events, or to make informed decisions about the appropriate course of action. This pattern can be observed in intimate relationships, for example. In one study by Fletcher, Fincham, Cramer, and Heron (1987), it was found that students in dating relationships who were actively considering separation, or were in unstable relationships, were more likely to spontaneously mention causal attributions when asked to describe their relationships, and also to report spending more time analyzing their relationships.

The principal argument raised by those arguing for the supremacy of a pragmatist model takes the same general form; namely, that laypeople are interested in the truth value of their attributions and inferences, but only at the sort of concrete, constrained level that would be of limited interest to scientists. For example, Swann (1984) argued that observers are usually more interested in predicting how others will interact with themselves, rather than predicting how they will interact generally with other people. In addition, he suggested that such a constrained orientation is usually quite adequate for the naive perceiver's needs, and indeed that the accuracy gained tends to satisfy pragmatic concerns. It is this latter claim that I take issue with here. For example, Swann (1984) wrote:

> Consider the fundamental attribution error—the tendency of perceivers to overestimate the role of dispositional factors as causes of the behaviour of targets. Because perceivers typically interact with targets in a limited number of settings, the situational forces that constrain the target's behaviour when they first encounter one another are likely to be present at later times. This is particularly apparent if one considers that perceivers are often one of the major situational factors influencing the behaviour of targets. The upshot is that perceivers who assume that a stable disposition caused a target behaviour, when in reality the behaviour was influenced by some aspect of the situation, do not err as long as they aspire to circumscribed accuracy only. (p. 471)

The question of whether such a narrow orientation will produce deleterious consequences, it seems to me, will depend crucially on whether laypeople are aware of the level at which they are operating. But the way the fundamental attribution error is defined, entails that people mistakenly believe they are producing global attributions and are not aware that they dealing merely with "circumscribed accuracy." Swann himself suggested that laypeople frequently conflate the two levels of analysis; for example, he claimed that observers are typically unaware of the influence they exert over the people they are interacting with. Now, on the face of it such ignorance seems more than likely to have deleterious consequences. For example, if I mistakenly assume that Fred is kind and loving and ignore the situational demands, I may make mistakes about the sort of person Fred is (Machiavellian and dishonest), and also fail to predict his behavior when the situation changes, as it often does in real-life settings.

A similar argument is raised by Friedrich (1993), who reinterpreted the so-called *confirmation bias* (attempting to confirm rather than disconfirm hypotheses) as a function of the central tendency for laypeople to avoid costly errors rather than seek the truth. I examine the confirmation bias later on. Here, I take up Friedrich's principal argument, with reference to his example of the employer who tests his hunch that extroverts make good salespeople by only selecting extroverts as employees. As Friedrich (1993) noted, by failing to examine the performance of introverts, "this represents a poor strategy for evaluating the literal truth value of the theory" (p. 299). However, he argued that the employer's strategy is appropriate because the employer is centrally concerned with selecting good performers and avoiding poor performers: "If most people high on extroversion tend to be good performers, it probably matters little to the employer whether good workers are overlooked because they are low on extroversion. ... Normatively appropriate data from introverts would have comparatively little pragmatic value" (Friedrich, 1993, p. 299).

First, a question: Why would the employer select as his or her hunch that extroverts would make better salespeople, rather than, for example, tall people or those born under certain star signs? Such choices will typically be driven by a more general causal theory that, for example, relates certain behaviors and abilities to particular personality types. And, crucially, the truth value of such a theory is going to determine how successful the employer is in selecting successful salespeople. If introverts make better salespeople than extroverts then the employer is in trouble. In short, success in avoiding costly errors is going to be intimately connected to the truth value of the underlying theory or hypothesis that drives a particular choice.

Now, this argument does not mean that laypeople can, or should, routinely test, or constantly agonize over, the truth value of all the theories they use in everyday life. The sort of research tasks and everyday examples that Friedrich describes often involve making a one-shot decision (e.g., Do I employ X or Y? What strategy do I employ to make a good impression or bake a cake?). In such situations the only rational strategy is to use the best theories one has available, with an eye on the costs and benefits of the possible outcomes. The fact that such day-to-day choices are routine does not mean that laypeople have no interest in the truth value of the underlying theories.

Yet another version of the idea that folk psychology is unlike scientific theory is raised by Wilkes (1991), who argued that folk psychology is centrally concerned with aims and objectives other than explanation or prediction (qua science). As Wilkes argued, folk psychology is concerned with such things as joking, jeering, exhorting, discouraging, blaming, praising, warning, insulting, evaluating, advertising, (and) hinting. The framework of folk psychology is a multipurpose tool, according to Wilkes, whereas science is a single-purpose tool being solely concerned with the aims of explanation and prediction.

One problem with Wilkes' examples of extrascientific activities is that some of them are clearly concerned with control (e.g., advertising and exhorting), which is also a bona fide scientific aim, especially in psychology. Still, her major point is surely correct; namely that laypeople use their "theories" for all sorts of purposes, many of which may have little to do with scientific goals. A good example of this is the way in which folk psychological judgments or theories are often used to assign blame or moral responsibility.

The main difficulty with Wilkes' (1991) argument is that virtually any scientific psychological theory can be, and often is, used for extrascientific duties (Copeland, personal communication, August 1994). For example, theories born and hatched within scientific institutions concerning the psychological effects of the weather, the food we eat, socialization practices, childhood abuse, brain tumors, or psychological disorders, are used within courtrooms and in everyday life to assign blame or moral responsibility. This does not mean that said theories are not scientific in nature.

The general conclusion I draw from this discussion is that a set of narrow or impoverished causal understandings of the social world will decrease the chances of laypeople attaining pragmatic goals related to predictability and control. Laypeople may indeed be pragmatists, but this does not imply they are also not realists, at times passionately interested in the truth value of their social judgments and theories.

Laypeople as Pollyannas

The thrust of this argument is that laypeople are more concerned with maintaining positive impressions of themselves and others, than in assessing the often bleak reality of their social worlds. That is, laypeople are much more interested in feeling psychologically comfortable than in searching for the truth. Supporting this view, there is a large body of evidence that suggests normal human cognition is characterized by unrealistically positive views of the self, exaggerated perceptions of personal control, and unrealistic optimism (for reviews see Greenwald, 1980; Taylor & Brown, 1988; but see Calvin & Block, 1994). Studies have found, for example, that 90% of business managers rate their performance as superior to their peers (French, 1968), most drivers believe themselves to be superior to others, even those who end up in the hospital after having accidents (Svenson, 1981), and most people believe themselves to be more intelligent and better looking than the average peer. As Myers (1993) put it, laypeople act like residents of Garrison Keillor's fictional lake Wobegon, where "all the women are strong, all the men are good-looking, and all the children are above average" (p. 91).

Moreover, it is commonly argued that this self-serving motivational bent influences the explanations and theories that people produce for social behavior (Kunda, 1987; Ross & Fletcher, 1985). For example, the well-replicated finding that people will attribute positive events to the self but attribute negative events to external factors is often labeled the *self-serving* or *ego-defensive* attributional bias (Ross & Fletcher, 1985). That is, it is assumed that the basis for such explanatory patterns is the motive to protect and enhance self-esteem.

In close-relationship contexts it has also often been noted that people are frequently concerned with justifying themselves and assigning blame, rather than dispassionately assessing the most accurate causal explanation (Fletcher & Fincham, 1991), and often appear to inhabit a world in which relationships are seen through thoroughly rose-tinted glasses (Murray & Holmes, 1993). In turn, these points have led to the suggestion that, just as in the individual context, lay relationship cognition is driven by the need to retain a positive and optimistic relationship conception (Murray & Holmes, in press)—more positive and optimistic than could be warranted by a dispassionate and rational analysis.

The centrality of the need to maintain a positive relationship account was apparently demonstrated recently in two clever experiments by Murray and Holmes (1993). For example, in Study 1, these authors first induced subjects in dating relationships to perceive their partners as rarely initiating disagreement, using a set of exercises that were structured to encourage this viewpoint. Then, this apparent virtue was turned into a fault by feeding subjects a bogus article from *Psychology Today* that stressed the importance of open disagreement and conflict resolution as a key path toward a truly intimate relationship. Essentially, this study engineered a lack of fit between their subjects' general theories about close relationships and their local-level theories concerning their specific dating relationships. Study 2 of this research followed the same pattern but focused on how insufficient attention to differences between partners is a major cause of problems in relationships.

In later questionnaires and open-ended descriptions of their relationships, subjects exhibited considerable fluency and ingenuity in reinterpreting and rewriting their relationship accounts that were clearly aimed at maintaining positive attitudes toward their relationships. For example, compared to a control group, subjects were more likely to both stress the way their partners openly engaged in conflict resolution and to construct rationalizations for their partners' failures to initiate problem-solving discussions, for example:

> On many occasions, I could tell that a problem existed, but she refused to talk about it, almost afraid of an argument ... *on the other hand, she is very receptive to my needs, and willing to adapt if necessary. This is beneficial to our relationship.*

> My partner never really starts an argument but knows *that if something bothers me enough, I will bring it up. However, my partner has come to realize in the past few months that the development of intimacy is important to me and he seems to be more willing to negotiate problems that occur.* (Murray & Holmes, 1993, p. 712)

The lay scientist model is not so easily disposed of, however. First, it is notoriously difficult to ascertain whether particular processes or outcomes are controlled by epistemic (e.g., truth-seeking) or esteem-maintenance values. In a seminal article, for example, Miller and Ross (1975) argued that researchers may not be justified in labeling as a self-serving or ego-protective bias the tendency for success to be attributed to internal causes, whereas failure is attributed to external factors. If people intend to achieve and also expect a successful outcome (as against failure), these attribution patterns could be rational outcomes of straightforward information-processing analyses. For example, if an individual expects to pass an exam, based on his or her ability and effort, then it is presumably rational to favor explanations for failure that focus on external causes such as the unusual difficulty of the test or bad luck.

The same interpretational problem can be seen in the research already described by Murray and Holmes (1993). The explanation offered by these authors for their results is in terms of esteem maintenance, in which the subjects' responses to having their relationships threatened were construed as clever post hoc rationalizations designed to retain positive relationship conceptions. But it is also plausible to view what the subjects were up to in quite rational terms; namely, as reinterpreting some aspects of their relationships, so that they could retain a coherent account that maintained a consistent connection between their general theories of relationship functioning and their attitudes and cognitions concerning their own specific relationships.

In the experiment by Murray and Holmes (1993), the cognitions that were engineered by the researchers to become imbalanced would be something like: "Our relationship works well and is successful," "Open disagreement and conflict resolution is important for producing successful relationships," and "Our relationship is relatively free of open disagreement and conflict." Now, there is evidence from this research that subjects focused on all three varieties of cognition in order to bring them into balance. It was found that there was an overall tendency for people to develop more negative impressions of the levels of intimacy in their relationships, that many subjects attempted to refute the importance of the postulate that open disagreement is healthy, and that others reinterpreted evidence from their relationships to emphasise the occurrence of open disagreement or conflict resolution. In short, subjects adopted a range of strategies to render their relationship theories as consistent and coherent.

Thus, subjects in the research by Murray and Holmes (1993) could be seen as motivated by a set of eminently rational and scientific values relevant to the construction of sound scientific theories, of the sort described in Fig. 5.1—for example, the need to explain and integrate apparently disparate pieces of evidence (providing *unifying power*), and the need for logical internal consistency and consistency with other accepted knowledge (providing *internal and external coherence*).

The work of Trope (1979, 1980) and others (Strube, Lott, Le-Xuan-Hy, Oxenberg, & Deichmann, 1986) is also revealing, showing that subjects will, at times, prefer tasks that provide good diagnostic information regarding their own level of ability, even when such tasks have the potential of providing ego-threatening feedback. For example, in the research by Strube et al. (1986), subjects chose to complete a test from one of eight different versions that all measured their general cognitive abilities. Prior to the choices being made, information about these tests was supplied to subjects that varied the extent to which each test version would reliably inform them whether they exhibited high or low ability. Subjects showed strong preferences for tests that were more highly diagnostic of their abilities, both in terms of low and high ability. In other words, subjects exhibited a preference for completing tests that were informative, even when such tests carried an increased risk that subjects might find out they possessed low general cognitive abilities.

In my view, the most plausible resolution of this battle between metaphors of the layperson as Pollyanna versus truth seeker, is that both motivational sets are often in play, sometimes at the same time, sometimes separately. Which motivational set is currently dominant will depend on individual differences and the circumstances. In short, the question becomes not which motivational set is correct, but under what conditions does each motivational set become primary?

In the close-relationship arena, for example, one set of conditions that determines whether laypeople predominantly seek the truth, however bleak, or simply try to hang onto rose-tinted view of their relationships, may derive from the developmental stage of the relationship. For example, it seems plausible that the need to produce accurate predictions and explanations becomes paramount when important decisions need to be made in relationships: Do I leave him? Should we get engaged? Do I date him again? Should we have a baby? How do I handle this problem? and so forth. At such times, the degree of commitment to relationships (and related judgments such as amount of love, relationship satisfaction, etc.) are precisely what are in question, so that the motive to retain positive relationship attitudes and predictions may loosen its shackles on the cognitive machinery. Alternatively, for couples settled into a comfortable maintenance phase of their relationship, such epistemic aims may seldom be invoked and the esteem-maintenance aims will be dominant.

Conclusion

Choosing between self-serving and rational social judgment models is, in the end, a fruitless exercise. And this is because both views are surely correct; people are both self-serving rationalizers and also scientists interested in truth and accuracy. Viewed in this way, the proper question becomes to what extent and under what conditions are lay social judgments determined by self-serving motivational goals versus epistemic goals? This kind of point is made often in the following sections.

Based on the analysis here, I think there is a good case that an important subset of the layperson's aims are similar to those of the (social) psychologist: truth, explanation, prediction, and control. The question of whether laypeople are hopelessly flawed in their attempts to achieve such aims is a separate and complex issue that I deal with in the remainder of the book.

HOW SCIENTIFIC ARE THE EPISTEMIC VALUES
OF THE LAYPERSON?

In this section I consider the epistemic values described earlier, and shown in Fig. 5.1: unifying power, internal coherence, external coherence, predictive accuracy, fertility, and simplicity. Psychologists have typically not treated these components as "epistemic values" per se, and they have largely restricted their attention to the factors of internal coherence (logical reasoning), and predictive accuracy (the testing and revising of hypotheses or theories). Accordingly, my discussion concentrates on these two epistemic values, and associated research literatures. I argue that seriously considering the possible role of the full range of postulated epistemic values raise doubts about the often negative interpretations offered by researchers of the layperson's performance in research tasks.

Internal Coherence and the Confirmation Bias

To test hypotheses in such a way that they are confirmed instead of disconfirmed is often thought of as illogical, or bad science, because this renders hypotheses inherently more likely to be retained than discarded. Indeed, up until the late 1980s it was widely accepted, on the basis of apparently solid evidence, that this is exactly what laypeople were prone to do. However, as pointed out by Klayman and Ha (1987) and Higgins and Bargh (1987), confusion has arisen with research in this area because researchers have often wrongly assumed that when hypotheses are tested by examining instances where properties or events are expected to occur or known to occur (a *positive-test strategy*), that this is equivalent to the adoption of a *hypothesis-confirmatory* strategy.

That the two concepts (a positive-test strategy and a hypothesis-confirmatory strategy) are independent can be easily shown; for example, to test the hypothesis that Person X is a schizophrenic, you may ask whether that person has recently suffered hallucinations or believes that he or she is the victim of a conspiracy (a positive-test strategy). However, this attention to positive features is consistent with either a confirmation strategy (attempting to confirm that the person is a schizophrenic) or a disconfirmation strategy (attempting to show that the person is not a schizophrenic). There is certainly evidence that laypeople favor a positive-test strategy in testing hypotheses (Klaymen & Ha, 1987). However, in research that has disentangled positive-test strategies from confirmation strategies little evidence has emerged of a consistent confirmatory bias in hypothesis testing (Farris & Revlin, 1989; Klayman & Ha, 1987; Koslowski & Maqueda; 1993).

Reliance on a simple heuristic, such as the positive-test strategy, can produce errors that resemble the confirmation bias. A good example of this phenomenon is the well-known four-card problem (Wason, 1966; Wason & Johnson-Laird, 1972). In this task, subjects are presented with four cards. Each card has a letter on one side and a number on the other side. The cards are presented in the following way: One card has a consonant showing, one card has a vowel showing, one card has an even number showing, and the final card has an odd number showing. Subjects are instructed to turn over the minimum number of cards required to test the hypothesis:

If a card has a vowel on one side, then it has an even number on the other side. Typically, less than 10% of college students select the correct answer, which is to examine the cards showing a vowel and an odd number. The most common responses found in a number of replications of these tasks are to examine the card with the vowel, or the card with the vowel and the card with the even number—both positive-test strategies (e.g., Griggs & Cox, 1982; Wason, 1966; Wason & Johnson-Laird, 1972).

Of course in everyday life, the sort of inferential task involved here (if P then Q) involves events that are semantically or causally related rather than symbols that operate as logical place markers. Further research has demonstrated that when logically identical problems to the four-card problem are framed using everyday tasks, then subjects' performance improves dramatically with a good understanding being demonstrated of the principle that to test the implication that P logically entails Q one needs to examine P and not-Q (Cheng & Holyoak, 1985; Griggs & Cox, 1982; Hoch & Tschirgi, 1983). For example, Griggs and Cox required subjects to consider a campus pub situation in which beer and cola is served and test the hypothesis: "If a person is drinking beer, then the person must be over 19." In this task, subjects are likely to examine the appropriate cases, P and not-Q (beer drinkers and those under 19).

A second example of research that initially painted rather a dire picture of the layperson's ability to test hypotheses was that by Snyder and Swann (1978), suggesting that people will ask leading questions that tend to confirm the hypothesis they are testing. For example, in one study they found that when subjects were required to test if another person was an extrovert they tended to choose questions from a prepared list that inquired about extrovert behaviors (e.g., "What would you do if you wanted to liven things up at a party?"); conversely, when subjects were asked to test the hypothesis that the target person was an introvert, they tended to select introvert related questions. Moreover, such biased questioning appears to lead to biased answers being given by the subjects and biased judgments being formed (Swann, Giuliano, & Wegner, 1982).

However, other research has shown that, under certain conditions, this apparent confirmation bias can be attenuated or reversed. The questions supplied by Snyder and his colleagues in their program of research were not particularly diagnostic, in that they tend to assume that certain traits actually exist. For example, the previous question ("What would you do if you wanted to liven things up at parties?") presumes that the person is an extrovert—this question probably discourages replies like "I have no idea, I don't try to liven up parties" (Trope & Bassok, 1982). Trope and his colleagues (Trope & Bassok, 1982, 1983) showed that when questioners have a choice they exercise a distinct preference for questions that effectively test the hypothesis under consideration, regardless of whether the answers are likely to confirm or disconfirm the hypothesis. And, finally, when people are given the freedom to formulate their own questions (e.g., Trope, Bassok, & Alon, 1984), for example when asked to test whether a person is an extrovert, they hardly ever construct leading questions, but instead, favor diagnostic open-ended questions (e.g., "How do you usually spend Friday nights?").

Predictive Accuracy and Other Epistemic Values

The final issue dealt with here concerns the postulate, often expressed in social cognition circles in the 1980s, that a general and central bias in the layperson's cognition is an unwillingness to modify or abandon beliefs, hypotheses, or theories in the face of disconfirmatory evidence (Fiske & Taylor, 1984; Nisbett & Ross, 1980). Such a conclusion could be taken to imply a lack of commitment, on the layperson's part, to the value of predictive accuracy.

The correct question, once again, is to what extent does the layperson ignore data that run counter to extant theories or hypotheses? In fact, the evidence concerning this issue clearly and overwhelmingly shows that the layperson's hypotheses or theories are usually influenced by data, as will become clear in the course of this chapter (also see reviews by Einhorn & Hogarth, 1981; Higgins & Bargh, 1987; Ross & Fletcher, 1985). The claim that subjects' performance is poor is not, however, based on the proposition that subjects typically ignore incoming evidence, but rather that subjects give insufficient weight to the data, and, hence, fail to adequately adjust whatever prior hypothesis or theory they possess.

The "correct" judgments, in turn, are invariably derived by researchers using either Bayes' theorem or the standard Fisherian analysis using significance tests. And, both of these normative models work by applying a straightforward mathematical theorem that assigns probability levels to the acceptance of the hypothesis, given the probability of the prior belief or hypothesis and/or the probability of the data. In short, the postulate that laypeople fail to appropriately consider new data, and irrationally cling onto their prior beliefs or theories, is derived from research and theorizing that embraces the kind of clear-cut algorithmic connection between theory and data, that I called into question in the last chapter. To recap, I argued that there was no such clear-cut relation between theory and data, and that it was by no means uncommon, nor was it irrational, for scientists to retain theories in the face of disconfirmatory evidence.

If it is accepted that the values listed in Fig. 5.1 are normatively appropriate in helping determine the plausibility of a hypothesis or theory, then consideration of them can alter the interpretation of the layperson's performance in research tasks, because psychologists typically do not take into account all the epistemic values that their subjects may be quite reasonably considering. To illustrate this point, I describe a typical research example concerned with people's penchant to retain beliefs in the face of contrary evidence.

Lepper, Ross, and Lau (1986) taught high school students to solve sets of novel deductive-reasoning problems with instructional films (described to the subjects as a species of mathematical reasoning) using either a highly effective or a thoroughly useless technique. As expected, the effective instructions produced much superior performance compared to the ineffective instructions. One group of subjects was subsequently provided with the opposite instructional film to the one they had seen, then solved a further sample problem (a discounting manipulation designed to allow subjects to understand the real impact exerted by the nature of the instructional film). The results showed that all subjects recognized the effectiveness, or lack of effectiveness, of the instructional techniques, although this awareness was more marked for the subjects who were shown both effective and ineffective instructional films. However, in spite of being aware of the impact of the instructional films, all subjects appeared to draw *unwarranted inferences* (to use the authors' words) concerning their own levels of ability at the task that were in line with the original experiences of success or failure, both immediately afterward and 3 weeks later.

One explanation for these findings, suggested by the authors themselves, is that subjects will seek to explain their initial performance and also seek to integrate this new knowledge with what they already know about their abilities. In the words of Lepper et al. (1986):

> This additional evidence may not only bolster impressions prior to debriefing; it can also help to sustain the belief after it has been attacked. When, as in the present case, that attack is less than totally decisive, ... subjects may minimize the challenge precisely because they seem to possess other evidence that suggests the wisdom of their prior conclusions. (p. 489)

If the list of epistemic values is consulted, this type of explanation implies that subjects are utilizing values of unifying power and internal and external coherence. Subjects' inferences in this study concerning their ability levels may be inaccurate, but they are not necessarily irrational or unwarranted.

As previously noted, there have been few systematic attempts to evaluate the extent to which laypeople appropriately use more than one or two of the set of six epistemic values described earlier in the realist model of scientific inference. One major exception is a study by Read and Marcus-Newhall (1993) in which explanations for social behavior were preferred by student subjects if they accounted for more data, were simpler, if they could in turn be explained by other factors, and if the same data could not be plausibly explained by other factors. In terms of the epistemic values described, these results provide evidence that laypeople understand and appropriately use the criteria of unifying power, simplicity, and external coherence, in the course of evaluating explanations.

A fascinating qualitative analysis by Planalp and Rivers (in press) of 76 people's attempts at dealing with events that challenged prevailing theories of their own close relationships, also supports the view that laypeople use a range of epistemic criteria when developing explanations. These authors reported that when relationships were important, and produced a lot of uncertainty, people behaved much more like prototypical scientists than they had expected. For example, subjects gathered extensive data by talking to others, sometimes tested hypotheses by altering their interaction with their partners, retrospectively examined past behavior for clues, and looked for explanations that resolved contradictions but were consistent with the overall relationship theory and related knowledge.

Conclusion

In conclusion, what evidence is available suggests that laypeople may well have an intuitive understanding of, and use appropriately, the set of epistemic criteria in evaluating lay theories or hypotheses. By focusing on the value of predictive accuracy, and ignoring the possible role that other epistemic values might play, psychologists have almost certainly underestimated the extent to which laypeople produce rational and reasonable social judgments.

Research results showing that laypeople will not readily jettison their prior theories or beliefs, when considering some disconfirmatory data, have widely been interpreted by psychologists as demonstrating the unscientific or irrational status of lay reasoning. The irony is that such results are, in fact, more reasonably interpreted in exactly the opposite light. Laypeople, like scientists, are inherently and appropriately conservative with respect to changing or abandoning their theories.

HOW SCIENTIFIC ARE THE METHODOLOGICAL RULES USED BY THE LAYPERSON?

Much of the research concerned with errors and biases in social cognition probably fits best into the Methodological Rules category, described in chapter 5 as a major component of the realist model of scientific cognition (see Fig. 5.1). The nature of this research has followed a common developmental sequence. First, some seminal demonstrations are produced that show people do not display a good understanding of such rules or principles. These findings then stimulate research that shows that under particular conditions, including in some cases quite minor changes in the way the tasks are framed, subjects display a good working understanding of the very same rules or principles.

I do not attempt a thorough review of this voluminous research literature, but focus on three areas that appear particularly relevant to evaluating the scientific status of lay social cognition: the role of base rates in social judgment, the so-called fundamental attribution error, and the role of individual differences in cognitive style. To anticipate my general conclusion, I argue that under unfavorable processing conditions laypeople do appear to resemble the cognitive miser model, which views human cognition as driven by simple heuristics and prone to bias and error, but that under favorable processing conditions lay cognition resembles much more closely the realist model of scientific inference already proposed.

The Role of Base Rates

Some of the pioneering research in this area provocatively suggested that laypeople pay little attention to base-rate information in forming social judgments. For example, Nisbett and Borgida (1975) presented subjects with descriptions of one of two previously conducted experiments in which the majority of subjects had agreed to accept a high level of electric shock, or had failed to help a person in need. One group of subjects was informed of these results and the other was not.

Subjects made predictions about their own behavior if placed in a similar situation, and also provided casual attributions, to either internal or external sources, for a hypothetical individual who had apparently voluntarily accepted a large and painful electric shock, or in the other experiment, had failed to go to the aid of a person in another room who they could hear through an intercom had suffered a serious seizure.

Presumably, knowledge of the base rates involved (most people voluntarily accept large electric shocks and do not help people who suffer seizures—at least in the research contexts fully described to the subjects), should influence subjects' judgments. Compared to the control condition (in which subjects did not receive this information), subjects should predict they are more likely to accept a large shock or not help the person suffering a seizure, and also explain the hypothetical person's behavior in terms of external rather than internal causes. However, the results showed that receiving the base-rate information of the actual results did not significantly influence either subjects' causal attributions for the behavior of a hypothetical subject or affect their predictions for their own behavior in the same situations.

Another much discussed example, is the experiment by Tversky and Kahneman (1980) in which subjects were told that in a certain town 85% of the cabs are green and 15% are blue. A witness identifies a cab in a hit-and-run incident as blue, and the court is told that in the relevant light conditions he can make correct identifications in 80% of the cases. The subjects were then asked what was the probability that the cab involved in the accident was blue rather than green. The well-replicated finding is that subjects make relatively little use of the base-rate information, the modal answer being around .8 (80%), whereas the correct answer according to Bayes' rule is .41 (41%). The layperson's apparent inferential deficiencies in regard to base rates have been explained in terms of the concrete, vivid, and salient nature of target-based information in contrast to the pallid, remote, and abstract nature of base-rate information, or in terms of reliance on heuristics such as representativeness (e.g., Nisbett & Borgida, 1975).

Following a familiar pattern, further research has shown that laypeople were neither as dim nor as inflexible in their information processing as these early experiments appeared to show. In the Nisbett and Borgida study, subjects were supplied (quite deliberately) with base-rate information that was almost certainly discrepant with their prior beliefs. Laypeople tend toward a more beneficent view of human behavior than is often revealed in the course of experiments carried out by social psychologists. In this situation, studies have shown that subjects are loath to accept the base-rate information at face value, and have a tendency to view the experimental sample as unrepresentative of the population in general, and hence not representative of the true base rate (Wells & Harvey, 1977). When it is stressed to subjects that the sample is representative of the population, Wells and Harvey showed that consensus information is used appreciably more.

Tversky and Kahneman (1980) modified the cab problem so that the base-rate information was presented in the following form: "Although the two companies are roughly equal in size, 85% of cab accidents in the city involve green cabs, and 15% involve blue cabs." The remainder of the problem was identical. With the problem framed in this way, subjects made considerable use of the base rates, in estimating the probability of the cab being blue, with a modal answer of .55 (55%). Tversky and Kahneman's explanation for this difference in findings to the phrasing of the problem described previously, is that the difference in base rates in the present case is more readily interpretable in causal terms; for example, perhaps drivers of green cabs are more reckless and undisciplined than drivers of blue cabs. In contrast, the former wording of the problem is expressed in a statistical relation that is not so readily causal in origin.

Other findings have confirmed the importance of subjects being able to plausibly interpret a statistical relation as causal in nature in making appropriate use of base rates (e.g., Ajzen, 1977). Such evidence neatly fits the lay scientist model, suggesting that an implicit, prime aim of everyday cognition is toward providing causal explanations rather than simply recording correlations between events in an atheoretical fashion.

Many other conditions have been discovered that can influence the utilization of base-rate information by naive subjects, including the accessibility of the information (Ginossar & Trope, 1987), the salience of the information (Manis, Dovalina, Avis, & Cardoze, 1980), the size of the sample the base rates were derived from (Kassin, 1979), and the credibility of information from any competing source such as the witness in the Tversky and Kahneman cab problem (Hinsz, Tindale, Nagao, Davis, & Robertson, 1988; for a recent review, see Koehler, in press).

Finally, I would add that it is not always clear whether researchers are treating the Bayesian model as a normative (Use_2) versus a descriptive account (Use_1) of lay cognition. Researchers often use a Bayesian model to derive the "correct" solution, typically assuming that subjects should disregard their own prior beliefs and base their answers entirely on the base rates provided. For example, in the research described earlier by Nisbett and Borgida (1975), it is assumed that subjects should ignore any prior beliefs they have related to the likelihood that people will help others in distress or accept painful shocks, and accept the base rates provided by the experimenter.

In terms of the model of scientific inference I have proposed, what subjects actually do is more consistent with "correct" scientific reasoning than what Nisbett and Borgida, and many others, have assumed is the correct normative strategy. That is, it is surely rational for subjects to critically evaluate base-rate information in light of their prior theories and knowledge. The error that psychologists have often made in this area of research is the same as that noted in the previous section, with respect to the phenomena of belief perseverance. The finding that laypeople are conservative with respect to adjusting their prior beliefs when receiving inconsistent base-rate information, is consistent with their reasoning being scientific and rational, rather than being unscientific and irrational.

The Fundamental Attribution Error

The tendency of the layperson to pay more attention to target information than nontarget information (such as base rates) led Ross to postulate the fundamental attribution error (also often labeled the *correspondence bias*)—the tendency to underestimate the casual role of situational determinants of behavior and overestimate the causal role of the internal determinants. That is, laypeople seem to prefer explaining an individual's behavior by leaping from the behavior to an underlying disposition—an aggressive action leads to an attribution of an aggressive disposition, a friendly behavior produces an underlying disposition of friendliness, and so forth.

One of the most popular techniques providing evidence for this "error" has been developed by Jones and his colleagues. In this technique, subjects read essays adopting a particular stance (e.g., for or against abortion) and are asked to judge the "real" attitudes of the authors. The well-replicated finding using this technique is that when subjects are informed that the essay positions were assigned (the authors had no choice) they continue to attribute attitudes that are congruent with the attitudes expressed in the essays (Jones, 1979). Subjects apparently fail to discount the effect of the situational cause (the instruction to write the essay in a particular direction) and assume the behaviour stems from an underlying disposition.

A plenitude of research has demonstrated the same kind of result in many different contexts; for example, even if one knows that an individual is instructed to smile and be friendly (like supermarket checkout operators), resultant attributions are likely to represent the individual as "really" friendly (Napolitan & Goethals, 1979). Demonstrations of the fundamental attribution error are favorites of social psychologists for laboratory or classroom demonstrations because they unfailingly work, and the effects are often large. There are also many real-life illustrations of the extent to which this bias can produce foolish or even bizarre human behavior. For example some people seem to confuse the characters played by the actors in TV programs with the actors themselves. There are many reports of TV viewers threatening actors they recognize in the street, on the grounds that the characters played by the actors have committed some dastardly deed, or of sending wedding presents to actors that have recently got married in their TV roles.

However, consistent with our previous discussion, recent studies have suggested that under conditions that encourage an in-depth and careful processing of the stimulus materials, compared to a superficial and casual analysis, correspondence bias will decrease (Fletcher, Reeder, & Bull, 1990; Gilbert, Pelham, & Krull, 1988; Tetlock, 1985). For example, using the same essay technique as previously described, Fletcher et al. (1990) found that elaborate in-depth processing of the essays reduced the level of correspondence bias, compared to a condition that allowed only a relatively superficial analysis of the same stimulus materials.

These findings are consistent with explanations for the correspondence bias that exploit the distinction between a characterization processing stage and an inferential processing stage (e.g., Gilbert et al., 1988; Gilbert & Malone, 1995; Trope, 1986).The initial dispositional inference (characterization) is regarded as rapid, automatic, and data-driven. This inference will tend to be linked closely to the behavior and hence will be more heavily subject to correspondence bias. The second stage involves more lengthy, in-depth, effortful, and theory-driven processing that typically involves a correction to the initial attribution, in light of the external constraints.

Individual Differences

As already noted, conventional wisdom, in the form of proverbs and fables, is presaged on the existence of individual differences in social intelligence. There is growing evidence that the conventional wisdom has something going for it.

For example, several studies have found that people who report enjoying intellectual challenges or have a low need for closure are less prone to the fundamental attribution error (D'Agostino & Fincher-Kiefer; 1992; Webster, 1993). Fletcher and his colleagues examined the role that the complexity of attributional schemata has in relation to the level of expertise exhibited in social judgment, using the Attributional Complexity Scale (Fletcher et al., 1986). This 28-item scale includes seven attributional subconstructs that vary along a simple–complex dimension, including the level of motivation to explain human behavior, the tendency to indulge in metacognitive attributional thinking, the tendency to infer complex casual explanations that are both internal and external, the tendency to infer causes from the distant past, and so forth. Initial results have confirmed that this scale possesses good internal reliability, convergent and discriminant validity, concurrent validity, and predictive validity (Brookings & Brown, 1988; Fletcher et al., 1986; Flett, Pliner, & Blankstein, 1989).

Using the Attributional Complexity Scale, Fletcher and his colleagues, and others, found that subjects who possess complex attributional schemata produce more accurate trait and attitude judgments than do those with simple schemata, but that such an advantage only appears to be manifested under conditions that encourage in-depth information processing that is goal driven (Devine, 1989; Fletcher, Grigg, & Bull, 1988; Fletcher, Rosanowski, Rhodes, & Lange, 1992). One explanation for this finding is that those possessing more complex attributional schemata will only produce superior performance when they are motivated to analyze information in an in-depth and effortful fashion.

For example, in one study (Fletcher et al., 1988), university students had a 15-minute conversation with a stranger under two conditions: as a personality appraisal of their partners, or as a communication exercise. Subjects then completed a set of personality ratings for themselves and their partners, and provided an open-ended description of their partners' personalities. As predicted, attributionally complex subjects, compared to simple subjects (as measured by the Attributional Complexity Scale), provided more causally complicated personality descriptions. In addition, complex subjects provided more accurate personality ratings than simple subjects (as assessed by correlating the personality ratings provided for the partners with the self-ratings of the same partners). However, as expected, both sets of findings were produced only within the personality appraisal condition; when framed as a communication exercise, the differences between the complex and simple subjects were relatively slight.

In another study (Fletcher et al., 1992), subjects who were either high or low in attributional complexity level answered either hard or easy causal questions. A sample of university students were required to solve 30 causal problems derived from Kelley's (1967) influential model of causal attribution. Kelley's model specifies that attributions are based on information from three primary sources: consensus information, distinctiveness information, and consistency information. The most clear-cut predictions from this model concern the informational patterns that should produce person, stimulus, or circumstance attributions. For example, suppose that John laughs at a comedian and I know (a) that John has almost always laughed at this comedian before (high consistency), (b) that John hardly ever laughs at other comedians (high distinctiveness), and (c) that almost everyone who hears the comedian laughs at him (high consensus). I should conclude that something about the comedian (e.g., he is funny) caused John to laugh. Alternately, a (a) high consistency, (b) low distinctiveness (John almost always laughs at other comedians), and (c) low consensus (almost nobody who hears the comedian laughs at him) pattern of information should produce an attribution about John (e.g., he has a warped sense of humor). Finally, I should deduce that something about the circumstances on this particular occasion probably caused John to laugh (e.g., consumption of alcohol) with a combination of (a) low consistency (John has almost never laughed this comedian before), (b) high distinctiveness, and (c) low consensus.

Now, in fact, there is a wealth of research that shows that people in general do make person, stimulus, and circumstance attributions in accordance with the examples cited, although subjects typically do less well on the Circumstance problems (see the review in Fletcher et al., 1992). This latter finding can be explained according to the difficulty level of the causal problems used in these studies. First, circumstance attributions appear to be more abstruse than person or stimulus attributions, involving as they do a casual interplay among the person, the situation, and the circumstances. In addition, the experimental items used to test Kelley's model are invariably framed in terms of a person responding to a stimulus (e.g., Mary is afraid of the dog). The nature of the description always suggests that a relatively simple attribution to the person or the stimulus is warranted—in this case either Mary is frightened of dogs or the dog is exceptionally fierce. In contrast, there is little in the event description or the usual accompanying information that would suggest an appropriate circumstance attribution—such an attribution would need to be imaginatively grafted onto the event description by the subject (e.g., perhaps Mary has just been to a horror movie that featured killer slavering dogs).

In this study, then, subjects who were preselected to be at the high or the low end of attributional complexity (according to their scores on the Attributional Complexity Scale) were supplied with 30 sets of information, via computers, that, according to Kelley's model, required three different answers (causes located in the person, stimulus, or circumstance) in equal numbers. In the "hard" condition, the order of the three types of information was randomly varied, and subjects chose their answers from the three types of cause, plus the four possible but wrong causal combinations (e.g., a combination of causes in the person and stimulus). In the "easy" condition, subjects were given the same sets of information, but the three types of information were presented in the same order, and subjects chose the correct answer from the three possible causes only.

The mean percentage of correct answers given are shown in Fig. 6.1, and the mean times that subjects took to answer the questions are shown in Fig. 6.2. As expected, differences between attributionally complex and simple subjects were magnified in the hard versus the easy conditions. Attributionally simple subjects did not spend more time on the difficult than the easy problems, and their performance fell away badly when answering the problems in the difficult format, or when dealing with the problems that required a trickier circumstance answer. In contrast, complex subjects appeared to control the amount of time they allocated according to the difficulty level of the problems, and, hence, their performance was less affected by the difficulty level of the problems. In summary, complex subjects handled the difficult causal problems as if they were experts, simple subjects as if they were relative novices.

It is important to note that these differences in performance between attributionally complex and simple people, cannot simply be put down to differences in IQ or academic ability. Scores on the attributional complexity scale are unrelated to verbal ability, IQ test scores, or other measures of academic ability (see Fletcher et al., 1992). An alternative interpretation is that this scale measures one important dimension of social intelligence. Truly, some laypeople appear to be better naive (social) scientists than others.

Conclusion

I draw several conclusions from this section. First, repeating a theme from the previous section, the research evidence clearly suggests that a prime aim of everyday cognition is toward explanation rather than simply the recording of relations between events in some atheoretical fashion: This is a fundamental point of convergence between scientific and everyday thought if the centrality of causal explanation in science is accepted.

Second, the general pattern of findings in relation to the confirmatory bias, base-rate usage, and the fundamental attribution error, are not idiosyncratic to these domains, but are typical of work in this area. (For reviews of this general area of research see Fletcher, 1993; Funder, in press; Higgins & Bargh, 1987; Kenny & DePaulo, 1993; Kenrick & Funder, 1988; Klayman & Ha, 1987; Koehler, in press.) In a nutshell, this research shows there exists a patchwork of conditions under which biases or "errors" are reduced or eliminated. In short, depending on the conditions, lay social cognition can look simplistic or complex, stupid or intelligent, unscientific or scientific.

Under unfavorable conditions that promote a casual, automatic, or data-driven style of information processing, laypeople appear to typically rely on fall-back heuristics or easily used rules of thumb. On the one hand, these heuristics are often reliable, adaptive and effective devices; on the other hand, they may produce characteristic biases or errors under certain conditions. However, under more friendly processing conditions, that provide useful cues or promote more in-depth information processing, these default heuristics tend to be corrected or discarded, hence reducing resultant biases and errors. These favorable processing conditions

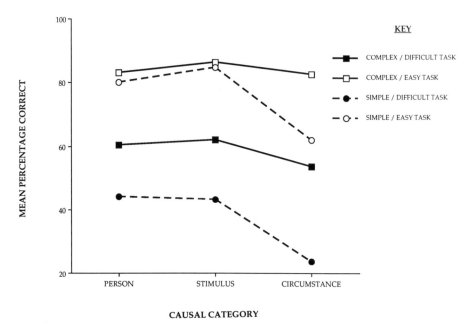

FIG. 6.1.   Mean percentage of correct causal answers as a function of attributional complexity, task difficulty, and category of causal problem.

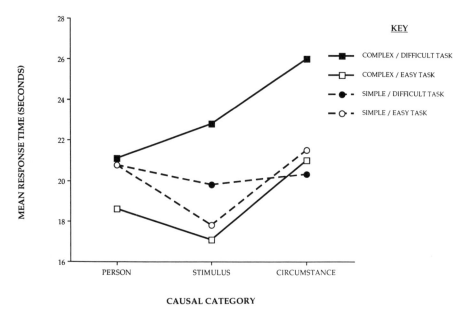

FIG. 6.2.   Mean speed of answering as a function of attributional complexity, task difficulty, and category of causal problem.

include adequate processing time, a light memory load, having the problem framed in a familiar context, having cues that help in strategy choice, possessing adequate knowledge or sufficient schema complexity to process the information, and being sufficiently motivated to carry out an in-depth analysis.

These conclusions in no way preclude the postulation of systematic biases or irrational tendencies in everyday thought, nor do I think that laypeople's competence in these matters should be established by fiat. However, I believe that one lesson of research and theorizing in psychology in this area is that caution should be exercised before concluding that lay cognition is irrational or in error (or for that matter the opposite).

Instead of specific inferential biases, a second kind of bias, that is consistent with my analysis, could be cast in general terms such as intellectual laziness or lack of self-criticism in the search for and use of evidence (see, e.g., Baron, 1985). Such biases entail that people are inclined to stick to the simpler and more basic processing stage outlined previously rather than move to the more effortful processing mode, even when such a transition would be to their long-term advantage. I have little doubt that such widespread tendencies exist; indeed, one function of our scientific institutions and norms, befitting their prescriptive status, may be to sustain a rational but difficult way of thinking against incipient human tendencies that all too easily lead to facile judgments being formed with subsequent dogmatic defenses of such judgments. However, the well-spring for both processing modes, I would argue, lies in our ordinary ways of thinking.

General Conclusion

In this chapter, I used the proposed normative scientific account to evaluate the scientific status of three components of folk psychology: its aims, epistemic values, and methodological or inference rules. In general, the conclusion is hard to resist that, under certain conditions, lay social cognition looks remarkably scientific. In the next chapter, I deal with the last component in the proposed model of scientific realism: the theories themselves.

Chapter 7
The Scientific Status of Folk Psychology 2: Lay Theories

I have argued in previous chapters that folk psychology can rightly be considered as theoretical in nature. If folk psychology is a theory, or a set of theories, then how should it or they be rated: scientific crock, touchstone, or something in between? The discussion in this chapter builds on the analyses offered in earlier chapters in which I addressed some critical issues concerning the nature of folk psychology and its overlap with the science of psychology. In this chapter, I use some of these prior analyses to help weave a course through a philosophical and cognitive science thicket of considerable density.

In the first section, I review the evidence and arguments already presented to the effect that folk psychology resembles scientific theories in some important ways. I then examine the question of whether folk psychological theories are mistaken (scientifically speaking), a perspective most persuasively and coherently argued by Churchland (1991), Stich (1983), and Ramsey (Ramsey, Stich, & Garon, 1991), and embodied in a position known as *eliminative materialism*. I argue that eliminative materialism is wrong, but that there are both important similarities and differences between folk psychological theories and scientific theories.

IS FOLK PSYCHOLOGY LIKE A (SCIENTIFIC) THEORY?

In previous chapters I argued, partly on the basis of psychological research, that it appears to be accurate and appropriate to describe folk psychology as consisting of theories. (The view that folk psychology does indeed represent a theory is commonly described as the *theory-theory*, a particularly inelegant neologism that means something like "the theory that folk psychology is a theory." I avoid use of this term.)

Moreover, folk psychological theories appear to exhibit many features that resemble scientific psychological theories. Consider the following list of generalizations that I think can be safely asserted on the basis of the argument and evidence presented in prior chapters:

1. Like one important class of theories in cognitive psychology (known as computational theories) folk theories of the mind seem to be functional theories. That is, mental attributions in folk psychology (to the self or others) gain their meaning and explanatory force by the way in they are semantically and putatively causally related to a network of goals, antecedent causes, and consequences (including behavior).

2. Folk psychologists appear to use their theories to achieve the same aims as scientific theories; namely, explanation, control, prediction, and the search for truth. This does not mean that folk theories are also not used to achieve other goals (e.g., to assign blame), or that all laypeople are always concerned with such aims. Nevertheless, these aims do seem to be an important subset of goals in folk psychology.

3. Like scientific theories, folk theories are often directed toward discerning underlying invariant psychological structures.

4. Folk psychologists seem to understand, and use appropriately, various epistemic values and methodological rules (at least some of the time) when evaluating competing theories or hypthotheses.

5. Folk psychologists, like scientists, are conservative when it comes to altering or abandoning theories on the basis of inconsistent data (although they rarely ignore such data).

6. Like scientific theories, lay theories are constituted at both the general level and at the local level. For example, laypeople have general theories about what makes close relationships function, and also local theories about how specific relationships work. Moreover, as with science, such local and general lay theories appear to influence one another in appropriate ways based on the goal of establishing coherence between the specific and the general levels.

7. Like scientific theories, lay theories seem to represent a structured and coherent system of beliefs, rules, and concepts. Lay theories are not simply shopping lists of causal propositions or concepts. A fundamental point about lay cognition, exemplified again and again in the psychological literature, is that laypeople are principally concerned with discerning underlying and coherent psychological structures located within individuals, structures that are perceived to generate and, hence explain, individuals' behavior.

In summary, I think there is an excellent case that folk psychology consists, at least in part, of theories that are similar enough to scientific psychological theories to warrant asking questions about their scientific credibility.

THE SCIENTIFIC CREDIBILITY OF FOLK PSYCHOLOGY: USE₁ VERSUS USE₂ REVISITED

Many of the arguments in philosophical circles concerning folk psychology have revolved around a position known as eliminative materialism: the view that folk psychology is a crock, doomed to be replaced by psychological theories with sterner scientific credentials (see Christensen & Turner, 1993; Greenwood, 1991, for two excellent recent anthologies that deal with this view). One of the principal and pioneering figures in the development of eliminative materialism has been Churchland. Churchland (1981, 1984, 1991) stressed that folk psychology should be evaluated for its scientific credentials "just like folk mechanics, folk thermodynamics, folk meteorology, and folk biology" (Churchland, 1991, p. 51). The evaluation actually offered is scathing. He claimed that folk psychology represents a false and radically misleading conception of the causes of human behavior and the nature of cognition. Folk psychology is held to "suffer explanatory failures on an epic scale" (Churchland, 1981, p. 76), and to possess a chimerical ontology—"Beliefs and desires are of a piece with phlogiston, caloric, and the alchemal essences" (Churchland, 1991, p. 65). In fact, remarkably little evidence is marshalled for such claims, a point I return to later.

Of course, the claim that folk psychology is doomed to be replaced by alternative theories is almost a harmless truism. Given that all scientific knowledge and theory is revisable, it is plausible that almost any scientific theory is likely to be replaced by a superior version at some indeterminate point in the future. However, to give this claim some punch, Churchland and other eliminativists have recently postulated that the overthrow of folk psychology is already upon us in the form of connectionist models that, it is argued, are fundamentally inconsistent with the theoretical architecture of standard folk mental attributions.

I believe that eliminative materialism is wrong. And, I buttress this view with four arguments that occupy the remainder of this chapter. First, the issues become clarified when the distinction between Use1 and Use2 of folk psychology is given due attention. Thus, I claim that folk psychology will always face the requirement of being built into overarching psychological accounts, in terms of Use1. Second, I argue that connectionist models are not in fact inconsistent with the folk theory of the mind. Third, I point out that eliminative materialists (along with many other philosophers) have operated with an oversimplified version of both folk psychological theorizing in general, and of folk mentalistic theories. If more elaborate and plausible descriptions of folk psychology are accepted, then the claim that folk psychology is, in principle, a scientific crock becomes difficult to sustain. Finally, I argue that an examination of the empirical literature in social psychology suggests that folk psychology is not as hopeless as Churchland has claimed. Each of these arguments is discussed in turn.

Why Folk Psychology Won't Go Away

Churchland seems to be concerned purely with Use2 for psychology as I have outlined it. Indeed, this is true for almost all the debate in this area, with one or two notable exceptions (e.g., Stich, 1992). Consistent with this point, Churchland often stresses the equivalence between folk psychology and other commonsense theories such as folk physics. In so doing, however, he runs foul of the argument I made earlier concerning that curious feature of psychology that marks it off from the other sciences; namely, that even if folk psychology is completely useless as a psychological theory itself (Use2), it will still feature as part of the content of an overarching psychological account (Use1). Moreover, as I hope the earlier examples concerning social cognition illustrate, this use of folk psychology is neither trivial nor unimportant. This fundamental feature of psychology is simply not true of other sciences such as physics or chemistry. There is no equivalent of Use1 in the natural sciences.

Thus, we apparently have a simple knockdown argument against eliminative materialism. Even if eliminative materialism is correct, folk psychology will continue to be analyzed and included as an important component (in terms of Use1) located within overarching psychological theories.

An obvious objection to this line of argument is that it entails that folk psychology will feature in psychological theories, whatever folk psychology might look like. For example, if folk psychology was to evolve into a radically different sort of animal in the future, it would (on my account) maintain a critical role in any overarching psychological theory. But one central question, so it could be argued, concerns the merits and demerits of folk psychology as it is *currently* constituted. I agree. However, to deal with this issue requires considering the viability of Use2 of folk psychology, a task I now turn to with an examination of the remaining three arguments.

Does Connectionism Mean the Demise of Folk Psychology?

The criticisms of Churchland, Stich, and others have been principally directed against the views of Fodor (1975) that beliefs and desires (or *propositional attitudes* as they are termed) are consistent with folk theory, and are best interpreted as functionally discrete, semantically interpretable states that play a causal role in producing other psychological events and ultimately behavior. Accordingly, the eliminativist set have fastened gleefully onto the recent development of connectionist models in cognitive science because such models postulate neural networks in which information is distributed across the whole network, rather than the traditional computational cognitive architecture that operates on discrete, functionally distinct, belieflike representations (as folk psychology does).

The first point to note is that there is a vigorous debate within psychology as to the merits of a connectionist approach. Interestingly, its critics tend to stress the extent to which the theory falls down in terms of its predictive and explanatory utility; for example that it is too powerful, predicting or modeling what humans can do as well as what are clearly beyond human capabilities (e.g., see Massaro & Cowan, 1993; McCloskey, 1991). Its supporters, in turn, stress the way in which connectionism offers a unifying model that is parsimonious and fertile (e.g., Seidenberg, 1993).

However, my aim here is not to discuss the merits or demerits of connectionist modeling. This is simply because the eliminativists do not base their arguments on the correctness of a connectionist approach. Rather their claim is that if connectionism is correct, then folk psychology is defunct (e.g., see Ramsey et al., 1991). It is not necessary to understand connectionist models in detail, to follow the principal arguments presented by the eliminativists, so my description of connectionist models is brief (for some introductions to connectionist models see Copeland, 1993, and Smolensky, 1988).

Here, I briefly describe the class of connectionist models that, according to Ramsey et al. (1991), are inconsistent with folk psychology (also see Somlensky, 1988). The diagram shown in Fig. 7.1, depicts the basic elements in such a model. There are two important points to note. First, such models are typically presented as cognitive accounts, not as descriptions of the neurophysiology of the brain (although the compatibility between such models and the neural structure of the brain is often cited as a point in their favor). Second, the entire diagram in Fig. 7.1 is at the cognitive level, including the inputs and outputs that are themselves cognitive representations.

Connectionist models consist of massive networks of parallel computing elements, each of which carry numerical activation values, or weights, which determine the resultant activation pattern and hence the output. The hidden units enable the system to learn how to perform a given procedure, without being told what functions to perform. Indeed, in research in which human capacities are emulated using connectionist modeling programs, the results are often so complex that it is difficult to tell what the hidden units are up to, or how the welter of weights functioned (McCloskey, 1991).

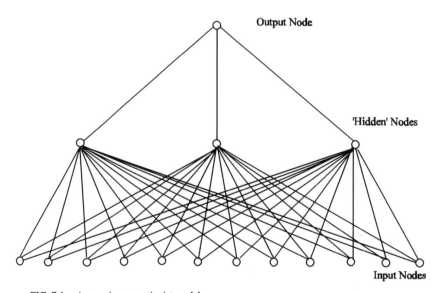

FIG. 7.1. A generic connectionist model.

To give a simple example, imagine that you perceived a stranger perform four or five honest behaviors (e.g., paying a fine, handing back some stolen money to a friend). Such behavior (coded as inputs) would have moderately positive weights that would presumably produce a dispositional attribution like honest. However, given that honest behavior is often rewarded or expected, external causes could also be seen as causing the "honest" behavior, which would mitigate against the attribution that the person is really honest. Next, you observe the same person commit a dishonest behavior (stealing some money).

We know from previous research (e.g., see Reeder, 1993) that such negative behaviors are weighted much more heavily in lay judgment than positive behaviors when it comes to moral attributions like "honest" or "dishonest." Hence, an output attribution like dishonest is the most likely outcome, with the previous honest behaviors being explained according to various external causes, rather than an underlying honest disposition. In a connectionist model, the introduction of the negative behavior would throw the system into frenzied activity, with the weights being altered until the system settled into a stable configuration, and the output could be read off (Fred is dishonest). In a standard connectionist account, this process happens automatically, simultaneously (rather than in serial stages), and information concerning the honesty or dishonesty of the individual is carried by the entire pattern of weights that determine whether individual units inhibit or excite the activation of other units.

The critical feature about connectionist models, in terms of the eliminativist argument, is that information in the system is widely distributed, rather than being local. For example, in the case just described, the belief (Fred is dishonest) is distributed across the whole network in terms of the weights. Hence, so Ramsey et al. (1991) argued, commonsense mental attributions like beliefs and desires do not exist as functionally distinct, semantically interpretable substates within the overall connectionist network.

In short, it is argued that if connectionism is correct, then folk psychology is defunct in terms of Use$_2$. However, I do not think the general argument is a plausible one, for reasons that O'Brien (1991) advanced, and that I explicate here. First, the conclusion drawn by Ramsey et al. (1991) that commonsense beliefs or desires are not located in particular parts or locations within a connectionist network is correct. However, there is nothing in folk psychology that prevents such mental terms from representing or being associated with entire activation patterns, complete with characteristic sets of inputs, outputs, and activation weights. Moreover, in connectionist models, such activation patterns are given the causal powers of initiating behavior or another network in the system. Finally, activation patterns can be, and often are, derived from inputs that are semantic and drive outputs that are also semantic in nature (words or sentences).

In summary, connectionist models seem eminently capable of sustaining just those features of folk mentalese that Ramsey et al. (1991) insisted are inconsistent with connectionist models; namely, that beliefs and other propositional attitudes are functionally discrete, semantically interpretable, and have causal status.

Ramsey et al.'s counterpunch to this move is that an important characteristic of many folk mental attributions is that they are dispositional in nature. In folk psychology, beliefs and abilities, for example, are ever-present, even when people are asleep. These authors granted that in connectionist models this dispositional aspect is captured in terms of what is termed the *connectivity matrix*, which is permanently stored, and generates specific occurrent patterns of connections between the inputs and outputs, along with their activation weights. However, as they pointed out, in connectionist models individual dispositions are not discretely stored in such matrices, but mashed together in a holistic fashion: "While dispositions to produce activation patterns are indeed *enduring* states of the system, they are not the right sort of enduring states; they are not the discrete, independently causally active states that folk psychology requires" (Ramsey et al., 1991, p. 115).

The problem at this point is that Ramsey et al. are imputing more into folk psychology than is warranted. Folk psychology is certainly tacitly committed to the claim that at least one class of dispositional mental attributions are mentally stored, that they can casually initiate other events, that they are functionally associated with particular patterns of occurrent cognition and behavior, and that they are capable of sustaining semantic interpretations. But, as we have seen all these propositions are eminently compatible with connectionist theories. Is folk psychology really committed to the further claim that the virtually infinite number of beliefs (including millions that have never actually been consciously considered or activated), that a person may be said to hold, are discretely stored in their own unique wrappers in long-term memory? Such a proposition is arguable at best, and implausible at worst. In my view, folk psychology is agnostic concerning such a claim.

Interestingly, it is also possible, and plausible, to turn the use that eliminativists have made of connectionist models on its head, and argue that the critical features of connectionist models make them comfortable bedfellows with folk psychology. For example, O'Brien (1991) argued that connectionist models nicely capture the holistic nature of folk psychology in that a multitude of beliefs or other mental dispositions are typically related in some background sense to a particular action or decision. For example, I might open the window in order to cool down, but this action is also related to my beliefs concerning the way window latches work, the effects of my action, the fact that the window was not stuck, that the air outside was not dangerously polluted, that there was not currently a hurricane in operation, and so forth. In this example, the innumerable number of background beliefs seem to work in connectionist models in just the holistic and tacit fashion demanded from folk psychology.

The same point can be made with respect to the sort of account that I have already presented concerning the way in which folk theories seem to be constructed of many different interrelated components to form scripts or prototypes, that themselves overlap in fuzzy ways. A connectionist modeling approach again looks promising in this context. Indeed, Read and his colleagues argued, for just these kind of reasons, that cognitive social psychology is an eminently appropriate domain within which to develop a connectionist approach to modeling social knowledge structures (e.g., Miller & Read, 1991; Read, Vanman, & Miller, 1995).

The Nature of Folk Psychology

One general problem with the eliminativist perspective is that it tends to treat folk psychology all of a piece, to be either completely discarded or exploited in terms of Use$_2$ as the basis for scientific psychology. Yet, folk psychology is a sprawling, ramshackle beast with a variety of organs—some bits may prove to be useful, whereas other bits may turn out to be of no use at all, or even pernicious.

The description of folk psychology in oversimplified terms is not confined to those arguing for the dumping of folk psychology. The entire debate within cognitive science and philosophical circles typically defines folk psychology in terms of the commonsense treatment of the mental, a move that leaves out those aspects of folk psychology concerned with behavior. For example, as previously described, personality traits comprise a central component of folk psychology.

In addition, the battleground over the pros and cons of folk mentalism almost invariably deals with a stripped-down version of the mental concerned with propositional attitudes like desires and beliefs. Again, important elements of the folk model of the mind is left out of such an analysis; for example, the attribution of emotions, and abilities or capacities such as intelligence (see chapter 3).

In chapter 2, I analyzed folk psychology broadly in terms of the content of beliefs and the underlying related cognitive process or structure. As already noted, the philosophical debate has centered on the validity of the underlying theoretical structure. But, psychologists also often use the content of folk beliefs or theories as assumptions or hypotheses.

For example, a good case can be made that psychological theories (along with the rest of science) typically rest on a network of assumptive beliefs that are quintessential common sense (see Fletcher, 1984). Among such bedrock beliefs would be included our assumption that the world exists independently (to some extent) of our perception of it, that the causal relationships that have held in the past will continue to hold in the future, that other people possess states of conscious awareness, that we are the same person from day to day, that logical deductions are correct, and so forth.

As previously noted, I would not argue that such fundamental beliefs be regarded as certain or absolute. On the other hand, there appears no reason, in principle, why psychologists, like other scientists, should not use such beliefs as the raw building blocks for their theories.

Folk psychology is also replete with proverbs and saws that express causal generalizations or principles of human behavior. To what extent such a knowledge base is viable or useful is another matter. But, again, there appears to be no reason why psychologists should, in principle, ignore such a repository of casual generalizations.

And, finally, a third way folk psychology can be exploited is through the borrowing of commonsense concepts and distinctions, especially those key concepts which lie at the heart of folk psychological theory. As already argued, this use of folk psychology is in fact endemic in psychology, with concepts like trait, emotion, motive, attitude, and so forth, being adapted and refined for use in many domains. Indeed, it is this particular usage which has been at the center of the philosophical debate about folk psychology, with the eliminativists claiming that propositional attitudes, such as beliefs, desires, and hopes, constitute the lynch pin of folk psychology.

Now, I would certainly not deny that propositional attitudes are an important element in folk psychology, but there are other key commonsense concepts that have quite a different definitional cum cognitive architecture, for example, emotions, ability attributions, and personality traits. I take the concept of *traits*. As previously noted, there is substantial evidence from the work in social psychology that confirms the importance and significance of this class of attributions in folk psychological theory. Yet, the theoretical outlines of such attributions appear to be critically distinct from propositional attitudes (Fletcher, 1993).

Unlike beliefs that are potentially infinite in their variety, in lay theory traits constitute a countable and limited category and represent rough families of behaviors, cognitions, and emotions that cohere to form stable patterns in given individuals (for more elaborate discussions, see Fletcher, 1993; Newman & Uleman, 1989).

Now, it is quite possible that propositional attitudes will bite the dust in future psychological theories, but that the commonsense concept of traits will live on, or that both concepts will vanish, but that folk theories of emotion will continue to feature prominently, along with the trichotomy of affect, cognition, and behavior (derived from folk psychology). Such examples could be easily multiplied to produce a long list of alternatives.

In summary, it seems to me that both the multifaceted nature of folk psychology and the variety of ways that folk psychology can be built into scientific formulations render dubious, at best, any attempt to in principle exclude folk psychology as a resource to be mined in the development of scientific formulations (Use$_2$).

I suspect that one source of the sweeping claims made about the inadequacies (or vice versa) of folk psychology is that, from Fodor (1975) onward, the debate has focused on the use of folk psychology within cognitive psychology: hence, the concentration on propositional attitudes that can readily be incorporated into computational theories of cognition (Greenwood, 1991). In retrospect, this would appear to be perhaps an odd choice. The domain in psychology that most assiduously uses folk psychology in terms of both Use$_1$ and Use$_2$ is undoubtedly, and by a country mile, social psychology.

The reason for social psychology's level of interest in folk psychology is not difficult to discern; namely, both social psychology and folk psychology are principally interested in the same psychological domain—interpersonal behavior. Social psychologists are interested in such questions as the causes of aggression, how sexual relationships tick, the contribution of personality in explaining behavior, why groups make the decisions they do, how emotions work, and how people build up personality impressions. So, too, are laypeople. Folk psychology assuredly contains a relatively elaborate theory of mind (Rips & Conrad, 1989), but perhaps the most accurate overall characterization of folk psychology would be as a *social psychological theory* rather than as a theory of mind. Bechtel and Abrahamson (1993) made a similar point, when they argued that theories in folk psychology principally deal with the relation between the individual and the environment, rather than purely in terms of a cognitive theory specifying mental processes and structures.

Moreover, as is already obvious from the previous chapter, and unlike cognitive psychology, a considerable amount of research activity within social psychology has been directed toward evaluating the accuracy and rationality of lay social judgments. In the next section, I summarize what this research tells us about folk psychology theories.

Evaluating Folk Psychology Theories

Before proceeding further, an important caveat is that evaluating lay social cognition theories in terms of their everyday successes and failures in prediction and explanation is not incontrovertible evidence in relation to the scientific credibility of folk psychology. For example, lay judgment might be flawed because of the limited access that people have to the powerful experimental and research techniques available to the research psychologist, rather than because of the barrenness of lay theories (i.e., the problem might be in the quality of the available data rather than the folk theories themselves). Still, an evaluation of lay judgment is germane to the issues at hand. If folk psychology is as hopeless as has been claimed, then it would be surprising to discover that lay social cognition (which relies on such theories) was immaculately rational and had the capacity to produce accurate social judgments and predictions.

In the previous chapter, I have already reviewed a good deal of evidence that suggests that under certain conditions, folk theories do rather well in explaining and predicting social behavior. With respect to the truth value or accuracy of lay social judgments a similar story can be told; namely that with increasingly sophisticated theories and methodologies being developed over the last decade, it is clear that, depending on the conditions, the lay perceiver has the ability to generate surprisingly accurate trait or attitude judgments of other people (Fletcher et al., 1990; Funder, in press; Funder & Sneed, 1993; Kenny, 1991; Kenrick & Funder, 1988).

To provide a recent illustrative example, Funder and Sneed showed to naive subjects videotapes of strangers involved in 5-minute interactions with others, and gathered personality ratings that were reduced to scores on the big five personality categories referred to in chapter 4: extroversion, agreeableness, conscientiousness, neuroticism, and openness (or intellect). Personality descriptions of the strangers in the videotapes were also gathered from their friends (used as the criteria for accuracy), and a different group of students rated the diagnosticity of 62 behaviors exhibited on the tapes for each of the Big Five traits. For example, speaking in a loud voice was rated as an indicator of high extroversion, whereas volunteering little information about the self was rated as an indicator of low extroversion.

Laughing frequently was rated as indicating high agreeability, whereas interrupting the partner was thought to indicate low agreeableness. The results suggested that for all the traits but openness, the cues that subjects used to form their impressions were valid ones that enabled them to produce remarkably accurate personality readings of the strangers shown in the videotape.

The upshot is that folk psychology works rather better than we would expect, if it was truly the basket case that Churchland and others claimed it to be. Of course, folk psychology is limited and flawed, and it would be foolish to expect that we could appropriate it holus-bolus as an overarching psychological theory. However, the body of research in social psychology is certainly consistent with the proposition that folk psychology is a valuable resource for theory building in terms of Use_2.

IN WHAT WAYS ARE FOLK PSYCHOLOGY THEORIES NOT SCIENTIFIC?

One theme running through this book has been that folk psychology may be more subtle and sophisticated than is often appreciated, and that much of the research and theorizing (of both philosophers and psychologists) may be, to some extent, vitiated by their often cavalier specification of the content and structure of our folk psychology theory. Being anxious to avoid falling into the same trap, I would allow there are some important and obvious differences between folk theories and the corpus of "scientific" psychological theories.

First, folk psychological theories, to a large extent, consist of tacit knowledge, whereas scientific theories are laid out in comparatively explicit detail.

Second, scientific psychological theories are concerned with a vastly wider range of phenomena than laypeople are generally interested in, such as the recognition of faces, the origins of nonverbal behavior, how language is processed, and so forth. As already described, the subdiscipline that comes closest to folk psychology is social psychology. However, even in social psychology, scientific theories range more widely than related folk theories, often dealing with issues and questions that go beyond the folk theories themselves (e.g., When do people indulge in controlled vs. automatic processing? How do general and specifically relationship theories interact in the generation of social judgments? and so forth).

CONCLUSION

The complexity of both scientific psychology and folk psychology perhaps explains the ease with which commentators can point to either critical differences or similarities in arguing how alike or distinct the two kinds of theory are. I have argued here that in important respects folk psychology theories are like scientific psychological theories, sharing the same aims, and possessing certain structural features in common (e.g., local vs. general theories, a concern with internal coherence).

However, folk theories also differ in important respects from scientific theories, in ways that I outlined here. For example, scientific theories are laid out in more explicit detail than folk theories—scientists can explain and describe their theories, laypeople in general are unable to do this.

In conclusion, it seems to me that attempts to either sanctify the central features of folk psychology or reject them entirely as a basis for scientific psychology founder on the myriad ways in which folk psychology and scientific psychology are related. Folk psychology is assuredly not inviolable, but I have argued there are good reasons for treating it as a valuable resource for scientific psychological theorizing.

Chapter 8
Summary, Caveats, and Morals

As already noted, attitudes toward folk psychology range from the reverential to the dismissive. I have argued in this book that both ends of this spectrum represent folly, and have instead offered a more moderate position, although one that has often defended folk psychology against its critics. In the concluding chapter the major arguments for and against the scientific or rational nature of folk psychology are summarized, and its potential usefulness to psychological science assessed. In addition, I summarize some conclusions about the proper use of folk psychology for psychological science.

ARGUMENTS AGAINST THE SCIENTIFIC CREDIBILITY OF FOLK PSYCHOLOGY

As is obvious by now, the arguments against the scientific or rational nature of folk psychology emanating from both psychology and philosophy, are many and various. However, they can be classified as falling into several types. One kind of argument takes issue at the outset with the claim that folk psychology consists of theories. Goldman, for example, postulated that folk introspective judgments are not theory driven, but consist of reports of private experiences or qualia.

The empirical evidence against the kind of simple introspectionist model that Goldman erected is voluminous, some representative examples of which I have previously described. This does not imply that private experiences or qualia do not exist, or do not figure in the self attribution of states such as emotions, beliefs, and so forth. However, I strongly argued for the view that such attributions to the self or to others are based on folk functional theories in which individual qualia are located within a network of other components including other mental units, goals, antecedent causes, consequences, and behavior.

Another variety of argument is happy to admit that theoretical formulations comprise a central component of folk psychology, but posit that folk theories do not resemble scientific theories in certain critical aspects. This kind of approach depends for its validity on providing plausible or accurate descriptions of both the nature of science and of folk psychology, which is one major reason why I have directed considerable attention to analyzing and providing an account of both sides of the analogical equation (folk psychology and science). Some of the arguments for the unscientific status of folk psychology, it seems to me, get folk psychology right but science wrong, some get folk psychology wrong but science right, and some manage the feat of getting both wrong.

For example, it has been claimed that lay psychology theories are irremediably local (referring to specific people or events), in contrast to scientific theories which are general in scope (e.g., explaining the behavior of people rather than specific persons). Another claim of this type concerns the way in which putative mental causes in lay explanation are closely linked at the conceptual level to descriptions of behavior. For example, to describe a behavior as an action, such as opening a door or saluting a superior officer, already implies an intentional framework that will invoke an explanation in terms of desires, goals, and beliefs. In science, it is claimed, causes and effects are kept strictly quarantined from a conceptual point of view.

The argument against folk psychology in terms of the local versus general nature of folk psychology and science, I have argued, gets both folk psychology and science wrong. First, there is compelling evidence that lay psychological theories are concerned with events at both the local and general level; for example, people appear to have sophisticated and stable theories concerning the functioning of close relationships in general terms, as well as theories concerning specific close relationships (including their own). Second, scientists are not just interested in general theories but also the analysis and explanation of individual local events (e.g., a particular earthquake or a specific murder). Hence, in terms of possessing an interest in both local, specific events and more general phenomena, folk psychology looks remarkably similar to science. In terms of the latter claim concerning conceptual overlap between putative causes and effects in lay psychology, I accepted this is true of folk psychology, but pointed out that this feature is also often true of theories in science more generally, including those in psychology and physics.

Another set of arguments focus on the aims of folk psychology, suggesting that lay psychologists adopt a largely practical orientation and are largely uninterested in erstwhile scientific aims such as explanation and the search for truth. I have no quarrel with such claims in terms of their characterization of scientific aims, but have argued that such propositions with respect to folk psychology are neither plausible nor consistent with a large body of evidence that show laypeople are frequently motivated by aims such as explanation, control, prediction, and the search for truth.

An analysis of the body of psychological research examining social inference biases suggests that one major problem with work in this area concerns the narrow, empiricist normative model of scientific inference typically adopted in the process of evaluating lay cognition. For example, in demonstrating that laypeople un-derutilize base-rate information, or are guilty of belief perseverance, researchers have implicitly assumed that the scientifically correct procedure is to completely abandon a theory when faced with disconfirmatory data.

If laypeople consistently ignored base-rate data, or did not alter their prior beliefs one whit, when in receipt of high quality data that challenged their preconceptions, then this fact would challenge the scientific credibility of lay social cognition. But research findings overwhelmingly show that subjects do usually adjust their prior beliefs or theories when considering contrary data, although they do not alter or abandon their prior beliefs in complete accordance with incoming data (as a narrow empiricist approach would dictate). If the kind of model of scientific inference that I have set up, in which predictive validity is but one criterion among others in evaluating a theory, is accepted then the finding that laypeople are conservative in terms of abandoning theories, and are subject to belief perseverance, is (ironically) evidence that lay cognition is scientific not unscientific.

The final species of argument discussed is known as eliminative materialism. Those presenting this position, such as Churchland and Ramsey, accept that folk psychology consists of theories that are scientific in nature (e.g., that folk psychol-ogy possesses appropriate scientific aims). Stripped to its fundaments, the eliminativist case is that folk psychological theory is almost certainly wrong or seriously inadequate, and hence is doomed to be replaced by alternative theories. Indeed, it is argued that the overthrow of folk psychology is already upon us in the form of connectionist models.

The former claim that folk psychology is probably wrong and doomed to be replaced is perhaps correct. However, given the inherent revisability of any scientific theory, the pace of scientific change, and the lack of any time frame offered (are we talking in 5 years time or 500?), the same claim could plausibly be made of any scientific theory.

The latter argument that connectionist models are inconsistent with folk psy-chology is based on a central feature of connectionist models that information is widely distributed rather than locally represented. Accordingly, so the argument goes, if connectionism is correct, then commonsense mental attributions like beliefs and desires cannot be mentally represented or stored in the fashion de-manded by folk psychology; namely, as dispositions that are functionally distinct, semantically interpretable, and causally efficacious. I thought this was a bad argument, and concurred with O'Brien that connectionist models were eminently capable of supporting the three features of folk psychological mentalism just noted.

FOLK PSYCHOLOGY AS A RESOURCE FOR LAYPERSON AND SCIENTIST

The general pattern of findings in the error/bias research literature shows that there exists a patchwork of conditions under which lay cognition can look stupid or intelligent, unscientific or scientific. Generally speaking, under unfavorable con-ditions that promote a casual or automatic style of processing, people appear to fall back on heuristics that produce characteristic bias and/or error. However, under conditions that promote a more reflective and in-depth style of processing, standard social inference biases tend to be reduced or even eliminated.

Research that has examined the accuracy of personality trait judgments, or whether laypeople are motivated by the search for truth or the desire to retain positive and optimistic views of themselves and the world, reveal the same mixed bag of findings. That is, under certain conditions the process by which laypeople make (social) judgments strikingly resembles our prototypical scientist. Such conditions include the presence of high motivation to produce accurate judgments, plenty of available time, and the possession of a sufficient knowledge base. Under other conditions (e.g., little time or motivation to produce an accurate judgment), or in contexts where other than scientific aims are paramount (e.g., defending oneself against a criminal charge, choosing a hat, impressing a friend), laypeople's thinking may not resemble our ideal scientist, but rather that of a typical lawyer, lazy thinker, artist, pragmatist, propagandist, and so forth.

Another noteworthy finding is that there are individual differences in laypeople's performance in social judgment (e.g., making accurate causal attributions or personality attributions), and in lay levels of enthusiasm and day-to-day interest in scientific aims (such as explaining people's behavior). In addition, there are strong individual differences in the kinds of lay theories that people develop concerning relationships, personality structures, achievements, and the many other domains of human behavior in which laypeople are interested. The wider culture assuredly provides the basic parameters of lay theories, the conceptual constituents from which most lay theories are built, and some sort of basic process model. Various examples of these general lay theories have been given in the book, including the basic folk model of the mind that we all share and use (see chapter 3).

However, within such general parameters, a rich smorgasbord of ideas and possible causes are offered in cultural theories; indeed, at a fine-grained level, several competing theories may be available in popular culture. From this shared base, then, individuals build their own personal theories, according to their own preferences, experiences, and skills, and so on. In short, folk psychology can be seen as providing a bountiful resource from which laypeople construct their theories. Folk theories, at the individual level, can be plausible or implausible, simple or complex, and can be used badly or well depending on variables associated with the individual (e.g., levels of social intelligence) and the context (e.g., time and motivational factors).

Folk psychology can also be seen as a valuable resource for the development of theories within scientific psychology, but just as with laypeople, a resource that can be used either badly or well. I have argued that the multifaceted nature of folk psychology and the variety of ways that folk psychology can be built into psychological science, renders problematic any attempt to in principle exclude folk psychology as a resource to be mined in the development of scientific psychological theories. It is equally important to resist the opposite, equally fallacious, proposition that folk psychology can (in principle) be safely used as the basis for a scientific psychology.

I have proposed that there are two basic ways in which psychologists use folk psychology—Use$_1$ and Use$_2$. Adopting folk psychology according to Use$_1$ treats folk theories as one component in an overarching psychological account that goes beyond common sense. This usage assumes that folk theories have a causal impact on lay behavior and cognition, but assumes nothing about the truth value or scientific validity of the folk theories themselves. According to Use$_2$, components of folk psychology are adopted into the body of the psychological theory under the assumption that the component is valid, or true, or scientifically useful in some way. I have given several examples of how these two distinct uses are at times conflated in psychology with harmful results.

Folk psychology is extensively used by scientific psychologists in terms of both Use$_1$ and Use$_2$, especially in areas like personality psychology, cognitive psychology, and social psychology. If it is accepted that folk theories do exert causal influences on lay behavior and cognition, then Use$_1$ is clearly legitimate, if not obligatory in domains where folk theories are alive and well. One important point here is that uncovering the nature and function of folk psychological theories is a difficult process that requires much research. The fact that psychological scientists often routinely use the very theories in everyday life that they are investigating, does not mean that this knowledge can be produced simply through introspection by the scientists themselves. The underlying structure and process of lay theories are typically opaque to the users of those theories—a fact that is not surprising given that lay psychological theories are typically learned and overlearned, through the lens of our culture, over many years of childhood and adulthood.

One important implication of the opacity of folk psychological theory is that commonsense judgments of how lay judgment or theories function need to be taken with a large pinch of salt. Take, for example, the question of how introspective judgments are made. As Gopnik pointed out, common sense suggests that we all know what we feel or think on the basis of some simple process of introspection. Yet, when the actual process of lay mental attributions to the self (such as attitudes or emotions) is examined in detail, it is clear that common sense has it wrong and that laypeople actually use sophisticated functional theories in which the experiential component is but one (highly malleable) unit in the lay theory driving such judgments. This kind of inconsistency is probably more widespread in folk psychology than in scientific psychology, and represents an important difference between the two classes of theories.

Whether folk psychology should be used according to Use$_2$ is a considerably more open and contentious issue compared to the question of whether Use$_1$ of folk psychology is a valid exercise. I have argued that there is no reason in principle why psychologists should not use the wealth of causal generalizations and theoretical concepts present in folk psychology. Folk psychology has been developing over thousands of years with largely the same goals as scientific psychology. Given the intelligence and intellectual flexibility of humans (compared to other animals), and our evolutionary success, it would be surprising if folk psychology turned out to be complete rubbish. However, this is a weak generalization that cannot support the adoption of any particular component of folk psychology to be included as part of a scientific formulation. The truth or usefulness of any scientific theory should be determined according to rigorous scientific analysis and argument. Whether the theory, in whole or in part, is derived from common sense is, or should be, irrelevant—that is, if we are talking about Use$_2$ and not Use$_1$.

I think it could fairly be claimed that many scientific psychological theories that have borrowed from folk psychology in terms of Use$_2$ have been successful in scientific terms. This does not mean, of course, that psychologists are obliged to adopt vast hunks of material from folk psychology, or that scientific theories that owe relatively little to folk psychology are doomed to failure. To borrow some proverbial wisdom, the proof of the pudding resides in the eating.

One of the key differences between folk psychology and science, already noted, is that folk psychology is infused with a good deal of tacit knowledge represented in terms of underlying structures and processes. Scientific theorizing, on the other hand, is committed to the principle that theories need to be laid out in explicit detail, including its assumptions or axioms. It is ironic, therefore, that one major way in which scientific psychology falls down, is in the way in which folk psychology is sometimes unconsciously or willy-nilly incorporated into psychological theories. I have previously given several examples of this process—for example, the way in which personality theorists have rather unthinkingly appropriated lay theories of personality structure, as they are represented in the English language, as the basis for scientific theories of personality structure.

The pervasive, taken-for-granted, feature of folk psychology is what makes it an inherently dangerous resource for scientific psychology. My own impression is that folk psychology is built into scientific psychological theories in a more thoroughgoing fashion than is commonly realized by psychologists or cognitive scientists. Ideally, folk psychology should be incorporated into scientific formulations in the same way as any other theoretical or knowledge base—in a critical and disciplined fashion.

Folk psychology (in toto) is not a full-fledged psychological theory, nor is it composed of full-blooded scientific theories. It would be foolish to claim otherwise. However, as I have pointed out, there are many striking similarities between folk psychological theories and how such theories are used in everyday life, and the theories and cognitive practices of psychological scientists. Given that science has flourished and been nurtured within Western culture, the close links between folk psychology and scientific psychology are perhaps not surprising. If nothing else, I hope I have convinced the reader that understanding and evaluating the nature of those linkages is an important task in forging a science of human behavior and experience.

References

Abramson, L. Y., Seligman, M. E. P., & Teasdale, J. (1978). Learned helplessness in humans: Critique and reformation. *Journal of Abnormal Psychology, 87*, 49–74.

Ajzen, I. (1977). Intuitive theories of events and the effects of base-rate information on prediction. *Journal of Personality and Social Psychology, 35*, 303–314.

Ajzen, I. (1985). From intentions to actions: A theory of planned behavior. In J. Kuhl & J. Beckmann (Eds.), *Action control: From cognition to behavior* (pp. 11–39). Heidelberg: Springer.

Ajzen, I., & Madden, T. (1986). Prediction of goal directed behavior: Attitudes intentions, and perceived behavioral control. *Journal of Experimental Social Psychology, 22*, 453–474.

Allport, G. W., & Odbert, H. S. (1936). Trait names: A psycholexical study. *Psychological Monographs: General and Applied, 47*(1, Whole No. 211).

Anscombe, G. (1963). *Intention*. Ithaca, NY: Cornell University Press.

Baron-Cohen, S. (1990). Autism: A specific cognitive disorder of mind-blindness. *International Review of Psychiatry, 2*, 81–90.

Baron-Cohen, S., Leslie, A. M., & Frith, U. (1985). Does the autistic child have a theory of mind? *Cognition, 21*, 37–46.

Baron, J. (1985). *Rationality and intelligence*. New York: Cambridge University Press.

Bassin, A. (1983). Proverbs, slogans and folk sayings in the therapeutic community: A neglected therapeutic tool. *Journal of Psychoactive Drugs, 16*(1), 51–55.

Bechtel, W., & Abrahamson, A. A. (1993). Connectionism and the future of folk psychology. In S. M. Christensen & P. R. Turner (Eds.), *Folk psychology and the philosophy of mind* (pp. 340–367). Hillsdale, NJ: Lawrence Erlbaum Associates.

Bhaskar, R. (1978). *A realist theory of science* (2nd ed.). Sussex: Harvester Press.

Bradbury, T. N., & Fincham, F. D. (1990). Attributions in marriage: Review and critique. *Psychological Bulletin, 3*, 3–33.

Brookings, J. B., & Brown, C. E. (1988, April). *Dimensionality of the attributional complexity scale*. Paper presented at the meeting of the Midwestern Psychological Association, Chicago, IL.

Bryan, W. J. (1909). *Speeches of William Jennings Bryan* (Vol. 12). New York: Funk & Wagnalls.

Bunge, M. (1991). A critical examination of the new sociology of science: Part 1. *Philosophy of the Social Sciences, 21*, 524–560.

Bunge, M. (1992). A critical examination of the new sociology of science: Part 2. *Philosophy of the Social Sciences, 22*, 46–76.

Burchfield, J. D. (1975). *Lord Kelvin and the age of the earth*. London: MacMillan.

Burger, J. M., & Cooper, H. M. (1979). The desirability of control. *Motivation and Emotion, 3*, 381–393.

Buss, D. M., & Craik, K. H. (1983). The act frequency approach to personality. *Journal of Personality and Social Psychology, 56*, 234–245.

Buss, D. M., & Craik, K. H. (1984). Acts, dispositions, and personality. In B. A. Maher & W. B. Maher (Eds.), *Progress in experimental personality research* (Vol. 13, pp. 241–301). New York: Academic Press.

Cacioppo, J. T., & Petty, R. E. (1982). The need for cognition. *Journal of Personality and Social Psychology, 42,* 116–131.

Cheng, P. W., & Holyoak, K. J. (1985). Pragmatic reasoning schemas. *Cognitive Psychology, 17,* 391–416.

Christensen, S. M., & Turner, P. R. (1993). *Folk psychology and the philosophy of mind.* Hillsdale, NJ: Lawrence Erlbaum Associates.

Churchland, P. M. (1981). Eliminative materialism and propositional attitudes. *Journal of Philosophy, 78,* 67–90.

Churchland, P. M. (1984). *Matter and consciousness.* Cambridge, MA: MIT Press.

Churchland, P. M. (1985). Reduction, qualia, and the direct introspection of brain states. *The Journal of Philosophy, 82,* 8–28.

Churchland, P. M. (1991). Folk psychology and the explanation of human behavior. In J. Greenwood (Ed.), *The future of folk psychology* (pp. 51–69). New York: Cambridge University Press.

Clark, J. M., & Paivio, A. (1989). Observational and theoretical terms in psychology: A cognitive perspective on scientific language. *American Psychologist, 44,* 500–512.

Cohen, J. (1990). Things I have learned (so far). *American Psychologist, 45,* 1304–1312.

Colvin, C. R., & Block, J. (1994). Do positive illusions foster mental health? An examination of the Taylor and Brown formulation. *Psychological Bulletin, 116,* 3–20.

Copeland, B. J. (1993). *Artificial intelligence: A philosophical introduction.* Oxford, UK: Blackwell.

D'Andrade, R. (1987). A folk model of the mind. In D. Holland & N. Quinn (Eds.), *Cultural models in language and thought* (pp. 112–148). Cambridge, England: Cambridge University Press.

D'Agostino, P. R., & Fincher-Kiefer, R. (1992). Need for cognition and the correspondence bias. *Social Cognition, 10,* 151–163.

Deaux, K. (1984). From individual differences to social categories: Analysis of a decade's research on gender. *Americdan Psychologist, 39,* 105–116.

Deci, E. L., & Ryan, R. M. (1985). *Intrinsic motivation and self-determination in human behavior.* New York: Plenum.

Devine, P. (1989). Overattribution effect: The role of confidence and attributional complexity. *Social Psychology Quarterly, 52,* 149–158.

Einhorn, H. J., & Hogarth, R. M. (1981). Behavioral decision theory: Processes of judgment and choice. *Annual Review of Psychology, 32,* 53–88.

Eiser, J. R. (1983). Attribution theory and social cognition. In J. Jaspers, F. Fincham, & M. Hewstone (Eds.), *Attribution theory and research: Conceptual, developmental, and social dimensions* (pp. 91–113). London: Academic Press.

Farr, R. M. (1981). On the nature of human nature and the science of behaviour. In P. Heelas & A. Lock (Eds.), *Indigenous psychologies: The anthropology of the self.* London: Academic Press.

Farris, H. H., & Revlin, R. (1989). Sensible reasoning in two tasks: Rule discovery and hypothesis evaluation. *Memory and Cognition, 17,* 221–232.

Fehr, B., & Baldwin, M. (in press). Prototype and script analyses of laypeople's knowledge of anger. In G. Fletcher & J. Fitness (Eds.), *Knowledge structures in close relationships: A social psychological approach.* Hillsdale, NJ: Lawrence Erlbaum Associates.

Feyerabend, P. K. (1975). *Against method.* London: New Left Books.

Fischhoff, B., & Beyth, R. (1975). "I knew it would happen": Recommended probabilities of once-future things. *Organizational Behaviour and Human Performance, 13,* 1–16.

Fiske, S. (1993). Social cognition and social perception. *Annual Review of Psychology, 44,* 155–194.

Fiske, S. T., & Taylor S. E. (1984). *Social cognition.* Reading, MA: Addison-Wesley.

Fitness, J. (in press). Emotion knowledge structures in close relationships. In G. Fletcher & J. Fitness (Eds.), *Knowledge structures in close relationships: A social psychological approach.* Hillsdale, NJ: Lawrence Erlbaum Associates.

Fitness, J., & Fletcher, G. J. O. (1993). Love, hate, anger, and jealousy in close relationships: A prototype and cognitive appraisal analysis. *Journal of Personality and Social Psychology, 65,* 942–958.

Fletcher, G. J. O. (1984). Psychology and common sense. *American Psychologist, 39,* 203–213.

Fletcher, G. J. O. (1993). The scientific credibility of commonsense psychology. In K. Craik, R. Hogan, & R. Wolfe (Eds.), *50 years of personality psychology* (pp. 251–268). New York: Plenum.

Fletcher, G. J. O. (in press-a). Realism versus relativism in psychology. *The American Journal of Psychology.*

Fletcher, G. J. O. (in press-b). Two uses of folk psychology: Implications for psychological science. *Philosophical Psychology*.

Fletcher, G. J. O., Danilovics, P., Fernandez, G., Peterson, D, & Reeder, G. D. (1986). Attributional complexity: An individual differences measure. *Journal of Personality and Social Psychology, 51*, 875–884.

Fletcher, G. J. O., & Fincham, F. D. (1991). Attribution in close relationships. In G. J. O. Fletcher & F. D. Fincham (Eds.), *Cognition in close relationships* (pp. 7–35). Hillsdale, NJ: Lawrence Erlbaum Associates.

Fletcher, G. J. O., Fincham, F., D., Cramer, L., & Heron, N. (1987). The role of attributions in close relationships. *Journal of Personality and Social Psychology, 53*, 481–489.

Fletcher, G. J. O., & Fitness, J. (1993). Knowledge structures and explanations in intimate relationships. In S. Duck (Ed.), *Understanding relationship processes 1: Individuals in relationships* (pp. 251–268). New York: Sage.

Fletcher, G., J. O., & Fitness, J. (Eds.). (in press). *Knowledge structures in close relationships: A social psychological approach*. Hillsdale, NJ: Lawrence Erlbaum Associates.

Fletcher, G. J. O., Grigg, F., & Bull, V. (1988). The organization and accuracy of personality impressions: Neophytes versus experts in trait attribution. *New Zealand Journal of Psychology, 17*, 68–77.

Fletcher, G. J. O., & Kininmonth, L. (1992). Measuring relationship beliefs: An individual differences scale. *Journal of Research in Personality, 26*, 371–397.

Fletcher, G. J. O., Reeder, G., & Bull, V. (1990). Bias and accuracy in attitude attribution: The role of attributional complexity. *Journal of Experimental Social Psychology, 26*, 275–288.

Fletcher, G. J. O., Rosanowski, J., & Fitness, J. (1994). Automatic processing in intimate contexts: The role of relationship beliefs. *Journal of Personality and Social Psychology*, 888–897.

Fletcher, G. J. O., Rosanowski, J., Rhodes, G., & Lange, C. (1992). Accuracy and speed of causal processing: Experts versus novices in social judgment. *Journal of Experimental Social Psychology, 28*, 320–338.

Fletcher, G. J. O., Simpson, J., & Thomas, G. (1995). *The structure and function of close relationship lay theories*. Unpublished manuscript, Psychology Department, University of Canterbury, Christchurch, New Zealand.

Fletcher, G. J. O., & Thomas, G. (in press). Close relationship lay theories: Their structure and function. In G. J. O. Fletcher & J. Fitness (Eds.), *Knowledge structures in close relationships: A social psychological approach*. Hillsdale, NJ: Lawrence Erlbaum Associates.

Fletcher, G. J. O., & Ward, C. (1988). Attribution theory and processes: A cross-cultural perspective. In M. H. Bond (Ed.), *The cross-cultural challenge to social psychology* (pp. 230–244). Beverly Hills, CA: Sage.

Flett, G. L., Pliner, P., & Blankstein, K. R. (1989). Depression and components of attributional complexity. *Journal of Personality and Social Psychology, 56*, 757–764.

Fodor, J. (1975). *The language of thought*. Cambridge, MA: Harvard University Press.

Fodor, J. (1983). Observation reconsidered. *Philosophy of Science, 51*, 23–43.

Fodor, J. (1991). Fodor's guide to mental representation: The intelligent auntie's vade-mecum. In J. Greenwood (Ed.), *The future of folk psychology* (pp. 22–50). Port Chester: Cambridge University Press.

Fodor, J., & Pylyshyn, Z. (1988). Connectionism and cognitive architecture: A critical analysis. *Cognition, 28*, 3–71.

Forsterling, F., & Rudolph, U. (1988). Situations, attributions, and the evaluation of reactions. *Journal of Personality and Social Psychology, 54*, 225–232.

French, J. R. P. (1968). The conceptualization and the measurement of mental health in terms of self-identity theory. In S. B. Sells (Ed.), *The definition and measurement of mental health*. Washington DC: Department of Health, Education and Welfare.

Friedrich, J. (1993). Primary error detection and minimization (PEDMIN) strategies in social cognition: A reinterpretation of confirmation bias phenomena. *Psychological Review, 100*, 298–319.

Funder, D. C. (in press). On the accuracy of personality judgment: A realistic approach. *Psychological Review*.

Funder, D. C., & Dobroth, K. M. (1987). Differences between traits: Properties associated with interjudge agreement. *Journal of Personality and Social Psychology, 52*, 409–418.

Funder, D. C., & Sneed, C. D. (1993). Behavioral manifestations of personality: An ecological approach to judgmental accuracy. *Journal of Personality and Social Psychology, 64,* 479–491.

Furnham, A. (1983). Social psychology as common sense. *Bulletin of the British Psychological Society, 36,* 105–109.

Furnham, A. F. (1988). *Lay theories: Everyday understanding of problems in the social sciences.* Oxford: Pergamon Press.

Furnham, A. F., & Henderson, M. (1983). Lay theories of delinquency. *European Journal of Social Psychology, 13,* 107–120.

Gardner, H. (1983). *Frames of mind: The theory of multiple intelligences.* New York: Basic Books.

Gergen, K. J. (1985). The social constructionist movement in modern psychology. *American Psychologist, 40,* 266–275.

Gergen, K. J. (1989). Social psychology and the wrong revolution. *European Journal of Social Psychology, 19,* 463–484.

Gigerenzer, G. (1991). From tools to theories: A heuristic of discovery in cognitive science. *Psychological Review, 98,* 254–267.

Gilbert, D. T., & Malone, P. S. (1995). The correspondence bias. *Psychological Bulletin, 117,* 21–38.

Gilbert, D. T., Pelham, B. W., & Krull, S. (1988). On cognitive busyness: When person perceivers meet persons perceived. *Journal of Personality and Social Psychology, 54,* 733–740.

Gilman, D. (1992). What's a theory to do ... with seeing? or Some empirical considerations for observation and theory. *British Journal for the Philosophy of Science, 43,* 287–309.

Ginossar, Z., & Trope, Y. (1987). Problem solving in judgment under uncertainty. *Journal of Personality and Social Psychology, 52,* 464–474.

Goldberg, L. R. (1981). Language and individual differences: The search for universals in personality lexicons. *Review of Personality and Social Psychology, 51,* 37–54.

Goldman, A. I. (1992). In defense of the simulation theory. *Mind and Language, 7,* 1–2.

Goldman, A. I. (1993). The psychology of folk psychology. *Behavioral and Brain Sciences, 16,* 15–28.

Gopnik, A. (1993). How we know our minds: The illusion of first-person knowledge of intentionality. *Behavioral and Brain Sciences, 16,* 1–14.

Gould, S. J. (1991). *Bully for brontosaurus.* New York: Norton.

Greenwald, A. G. (1980). The totalitarian ego: Fabrication and revision of personal history. *American Psychologist, 35,* 603–618.

Greenwood, J. D. (1989). *Explanation and experiment in social psychological science.* New York: Springer Verlag.

Greenwood, J. D. (Ed.). (1991). *The future of folk psychology.* New York: Cambridge University Press.

Greenwood, J. D. (1992). Realism, empiricism, and social constructionism. *Theory and Psychology, 2,* 131–151.

Griggs, R. A., & Cox, J. R. (1982). The elusive thematic—Materials effect in Wason's selection task. *British Journal of Psychology, 73,* 407–420.

Haldane, J. (1988). Understanding folk. *Proceedings of the Aristofelian Society (Suppl.), 62,* 222–246.

Hare-Mustin, R. T., & Marecek, J. (1988). The meaning of difference: Gender theory, postmodernism, and psychology. *American Psychologist, 43,* 455–464.

Harré, R. (1989). Metaphysics and methodology: Some prescriptions for social psychological research. *European Journal of Social Psychology, 19,* 439–454.

Heider, F. (1958). *The psychology of interpersonal relations.* New York: Wiley.

Hewstone, M. (1989). *Causal attribution: From cognitive processes to collective beliefs.* Oxford: Basil Blackwell.

Higgins, E. T., & Bargh, J. A. (1987). Social cognition and social perception. *Annual Review of Psychology, 38,* 369–425.

Hinsz, V. B., Tindale, R. S., Nagao, D. H., Davis, J. H., & Robertson, B. A. (1988). The influence of the accuracy of individuating information on the use of base rate information in probability judgment. *Journal of Experimental Social Psychology, 24,* 127–145.

Hoch, S. J., & Tschirgi, J. E. (1983). Cue redundancy and extra logical inference in a deductive reasoning task. *Memory and Cognition, 11,* 200–209.

Holyoak, K. J., & Spellman, B. A. (1993). Thinking. *Annual Review of Psychology, 44,* 265–315.

Hooker, C. A. (1987). *A realistic theory of science.* New York: State University of New York Press.

Horgan, J. (1992, July). Quantum philosophy. *Scientific American,* pp. 72–80.

Howard, G. S. (1985). The role of values in the science of psychology. *American Psychologist, 40,* 255–265.

Hume, D. (1962). An inquiry concerning human understanding, 1777. In L.A. Selby-Bigge (Ed.), *Hume's enquiries* (pp. 5–165). Oxford, England: Clarendon Press.

Jabs, A. (1992). An interpretation of the formalism of quantum mechanics in terms of epistemological realism. *British Journal for the Philosophy of Science, 43,* 405–421.

Johnson-Laird, P. N., & Oatley, K. (1989). The language of emotions: An analysis of a semantic field. *Cognition and Emotion, 3,* 81–123.

Jones, E. E. (1979). The rocky road from acts to dispositions. *American Psychologist, 34,* 107–117.

Kassin, S. M. (1979). Base rates and prediction: The role of sample size. *Personality and Social Psychology Bulletin, 5,* 210–213.

Kelley, H. H. (1967). Attribution theory in social psychology. In D. L. Vine (Ed.), *Nebraska symposium on motivation* (pp. 192–238). Lincoln: University of Nebraska Press.

Kelley, H. H. (1991). Common-sense psychology and scientific psychology. *Annual Review of Psychology, 43,* 1–23.

Kelley, H. H. (1992). Common-sense psychology and scientific psychology. *Annual Review of Psychology, 43,* 1–23.

Kenny, D. A. (1991). A general model of consensus and accuracy in interpersonal perception. *Psychological Review, 98,* 155–164.

Kenny, D. A., & DePaulo, B. M. (1993). Do people know how others view them? An empirical and theoretical account. *Psychological Bulletin, 114,* 145–161.

Kenrick, D. T., & Funder, D. C. (1988). Profiting from controversy: Lessons from the person-situation debate. *American Psychologist, 43,* 23–34.

Kimble, G. A. (1989). Psychology from the standpoint of the generalist. *American Psychologist, 44,* 491–499.

Klayman, J., & Ha, Y. W. (1987). Confirmation, disconfirmation, and information in hypothesis testing. *Psychological Review, 94,* 211–228.

Koehler, J. J. (in press). The base rate fallacy reconsidered: Descriptive, normative, and methodological challenges. *Behavioral and Brain Sciences.*

Koslowski, B., & Maqueda, M. (1993). What is confirmation bias and when do people actually have it? *Merrill Palmer Quarterly, 39,* 104–130.

Kuhn, T. S. (1962). *The structure of scientific revolutions* (1st ed.). Chicago: University of Chicago Press.

Kuhn, T. S. (1970). *The structure of scientific revolutions* (2nd rev. ed.). Chicago: University of Chicago Press.

Kunda, Z. (1987). Motivated inference: Self-serving generation and evaluation of causal theories. *Journal of Personality and Social Psychology, 53,* 636–647.

Laudan, L. (1984). *Science and values: An essay on the aims of science and their role in scientific debate.* Berkeley: University of California Press.

Lepper, M. R., Ross, L., & Lau, R. R. (1986). Persistence in inaccurate beliefs about the self: Perseverance effects in the classroom. *Journal of Personality and Social Psychology, 50,* 482–491.

MacCorquodale, K., & Meehl, P. E. (1948). On a distinction between hypothetical constructs and intervening variables. *Psychological Review, 55,* 95–107.

Manicas, P. T., & Secord, P. F. (1983). Implications for psychology of the new philosophy of science. *American Psychologist, 38,* 399–413.

Manis, M., Dovalina, I., Avis, N. E., Cardoze, S. (1980). Base rates can affect individual predictions. *Journal of Personality and Social Psychology, 38,* 231–248.

Massaro, D. W., & Cowan, N. (1993). Information processing models: Microscopes of the mind. *Annual Review of Psychology, 44,* 383–425.

McCloskey, M. (1991). Networks and theories: The place of connectionism in cognitive science. *Psychological Science, 2,* 387–395.

McCrae, R. R., & Costa, P. T. (1985). Updating Norman's "adequate taxonomy": Intelligence and personality dimensions in natural language and in questionnaires. *Journal of Personality and Social Psychology, 49,* 710–721.

McGuire, W. J. (1985). Attitudes and attitude change. In G. Lindzey & E. Aronson (Eds.), *The handbook of social psychology* (3rd ed., pp. 223–346). New York: Random House.

McMullin, E. (1983). Values in science. In P. D. Asquith & T. Nickles (Eds.), *Proceedings of the 1982 Philosophy of Science Association* (Vol. 2, pp. 3–23). East Lansing, MI: Philosophy of Science Association.

McMullin, E. (1984). A case for scientific realism. In J. Leplin (Ed.), *Essays on scientific realism* (pp. 53–71). Los Angeles: University of California Press.

Medvedev, Z. A. (1969). *The rise and fall of T.D. Lysenko*. New York: Columbia University Press.

Miller, D. T., & Ross, M. (1975). Self-serving biases in the attribution of causality: Fact or fiction? *Psychological Bulletin, 82*, 213–225.

Miller, L. C., & Read, S. J. (1991). On the coherence of mental models of persons and relationships: A knowledge structure approach. In G. J. O. Fletcher & F. D. Fincham (Eds.), *Cognition in close relationships* (pp 69–100). Hillsdale, NJ: Lawrence Erlbaum Associates.

Moscovici, S. (1976). *La Psychanalyse: Son image et son public*. Paris: Presses Universitaires de France. (Original work published 1961)

Murray, S. L., & Holmes, J. G. (1993). Seeing virtues in faults: Negativity and the transformation of interpersonal narratives in close relationships. *Journal of Personality and Social Psychology, 61*, 707–721.

Murray, S., & Holmes, J. (in press). The construction of relationship realities. In G. Fletcher & J. Fitness (Eds.), *Knowledge structures in close relationships: A social psychological approach*. Hillsdale, NJ: Lawrence Erlbaum Associates.

Myers, D. G. (1993). *Social psychology* (4th ed.). New York: McGraw-Hill.

Napolitan, D. A., & Goethals, G. R. (1979). The attribution of friendliness. *Journal of Experimental Social Psychology, 15*, 105–113.

Newman, L. S., & Uleman, J. S. (1989). Spontaneous trait inference. In J. S. Uleman & J. A. Bargh (Eds.), *Unintended thought* (pp. 155–187). New York: Guilford Press.

Nisbett, R. E., & Borgida, E. (1975). Attribution and the psychology of prediction. *Journal of Personality and Social Psychology, 32*, 932–943.

Nisbett, R. E., & Ross, L. (1980). *Human inference: Strategies and shortcomings of social judgment*. Englewood Cliffs, NJ: Prentice-Hall.

Norman, W. T. (1963). Toward an adequate taxonomy of personality attributes: Replicated factor structure in peer nomination personality ratings. *Journal of Abnormal and Social Psychology, 66*, 574–583.

Norris, C. (1991). *Deconstructionism: Theory and practice* (rev. ed.). New York: Routledge.

O'Brien, G. (1991). Is connectionism commonsense? *Philosophical Psychology, 4*, 165–181.

Park, B. (1986). A method for studying the development of impressions of real people. *Journal of Personality and Social Psychology, 51*(5), 907–917.

Peters, R. S. (1960). *The concept of motivation* (2nd ed). London: Routledge & Kegan Paul.

Planalp, S., & Rivers, M. (in press). Changes in knowledge of personal relationships. In G. Fletcher & J. Fitness (Eds.), *Knowledge structures in close relationships: A social psychological approach*. Hillsdale, NJ: Lawrence Erlbaum Associates.

Popper, K. (1959). *The logic of scientific discovery*. London: Hutchinson. (Original work published 1935)

Potter, J., & Wetherell, M. (1987). *Discourse and social psychology: Beyond attitudes and behaviour*. London: Sage.

Pylyshyn, Z. (1980). Computation and cognition. Issues in the foundations of cognitive science. *Behavioral and Brain Science, 3*, 111–132.

Ramsey, W., Stich, S., & Garon, J. (1991). Connectionism, eliminativism, and the future of folk psychology. In J. D. Greenwood (Ed.), *The future of folk psychology* (pp. 93–119). Cambridge: Cambridge University Press.

Read, S. J., & Marcos-Newhall, A. (1993). Explanatory coherence in social explanations: A parallel distributed processing account. *Journal of Personality and Social Psychology, 65, 429–447*.

Read, S. J., Vanman, E. J., & Miller, L. C. (1995). *Parallel constraint satisfaction processes and Gestalt principles: (Re) introducing cognitive dynamics to social psychology*. Unpublished manuscript, Department of Psychology, University of Southern California, Los Angeles.

Reeder, G. D. (1993). Trait—behavior relations and dispostional inference. *Personality and Social Psychology Bulletin, 19*, 586–593.

Riger, S. (1992). Epistemological debates, feminist voices: Science, social values, and the study of women. *American Psychologist, 47*, 730–740.

Rippere, V. (1977). Common sense beliefs about depression and anti-depressive behaviour: A study of social consensus. *Behaviour Research and Therapy, 15*, 465–470.

Rips, L. J., & Conrad, F. G. (1989). Folk psychology of mental activities. *Psychological Review, 96*, 187–207.

Rogers, T. B. (1990). Proverbs as psychological theories … Or is it the other way around? *Canadian Psychology, 31*, 195–207.

Rosch, E. (1978). Principles of categorization. In E. Rosch & B. B. Lloyd (Eds)., *Cognition and categorization* (pp. 27–48). Hillsdale, NJ: Lawrence Erlbaum Associates.

Rosnow, R. L., & Rosenthal, R. (1989). Statistical procedures and the justification of knowledge in psychological science. *American Psychologist, 44*, 1276–1284.

Ross, L. (1977). The intuitive psychologist and his shortcomings: Distortions in the attribution process. In L. Berkowitz (Ed.), *Advances in experimental social psychology* (Vol. 10, pp. 173–220). New York: Academic Press.

Ross, M., & Fletcher, G, J. O. (1985). Attribution and social perception. In G. Lindzey & E. Aronson (Eds.), *The handbook of social psychology* (3rd ed., pp. 73–122). New York: Random House.

Ross, M., McFarland, C., & Fletcher, G. J. O. (1981). The effect of attitude on the recall of personal histories. *Journal of Personality and Social Psychology, 40*, 627–634.

Rothbart, M., & Park, B. (1986). As the confirmability and disconfirmability of trait concepts. *Journal of Personality and Social Psychology, 50*, 131–142.

Russell, J. A. (1991). In defense of a prototype approach to emotion concepts. *Journal of Personality and Social Psychology, 60*, 37–47.

Searle, J. (1980). The intentionality of intention and action. *Cognitive Science, 4,* 47–70.

Sedikides, C., & Anderson, C. A. (1994). Causal perceptions of intertrait relations: The glue that hold person types together. *Personality and Social Psychology Bulletin, 20*, 294–302.

Seidenberg, M. S. (1993). Connectionist models and cognitive theory. *Psychological Science, 4*, 228–235.

Seligman, M. E. P. (1991). *Learned optimism.* New York: Knopf.

Semin, G. R., & Krahe, B. (1987). Lay conceptions of personality: Eliciting tiers of a scientific conception of personality. *European Journal of Social Psychology, 17*, 199–209.

Shaver, K. G. (1985). *The attribution of blame: Causality, responsibility, and blameworthiness.* New York: Springer-Verlag.

Shaver, K. G., & Drown, D. (1986). On causality, responsibility, and self-blame: A theoretical note. *Journal of Personality and Social Psychology, 50*, 697–702.

Shiffrin, R. M., & Schneider, W. (1984). Automatic and controlled processing revisited. *Psychological Review, 91*, 269–276.

Shotter, J. (1984). *Social accountability and selfhood.* Oxford: Blackwell.

Siegel, H. (1987). *Relativism refuted: A critique of contemporary methodological relativism.* Boston: Reidel.

Silverman, H. (Ed.). (1990). *Postmodernism—Philosophy and the arts.* London: Routledge.

Skinner, B. F. (1974). *About behaviorism.* New York: Knopf.

Skinner, B. F. (1978). *Reflections on behaviorism and society.* Englewood Cliffs, NJ: Prentice-Hall.

Smolensky, P. (1988). On the proper treatment of connectionism. *Behavioral and Brain Sciences, 11,* 1–74.

Snyder, M., & Swann, W. B., Jr. (1978). Hypothesis—testing in social interaction. *Journal of Personality and Social Psychology, 36*, 1202–1212.

Staats, A. W. (1991). Unified positivism and unification psychology: Fad or new field? *American Psychologist, 46*, 899–912.

Sternberg, R. J., Conway, B. E., Ketron, J. L., & Bernstein, M. (1981). People's conception of intelligence. *Journal of Personality and Social Psychology, 41*, 37–55.

Stich, S. P. (1983). *From folk psychology to cognitive science: The case against belief.* Cambridge, MA: MIT Press.

Stich, S. P. (1992). What is a theory of mental representation? *Mind, 101*, 243–261.

Strongman, K. (1987). *The psychology of emotion* (3rd ed.). Chichester, England: Wiley.

Strube, M. J., Lott, C. L., Le-Xuan-Hy, G. M., Oxenberg, J., & Deichmann, A. K. (1986). Self-evaluation of abilities: Accurate self-assessment versus biased self-enhancement. *Journal of Personality and Social Psychology, 51,* 16–25.

Svenson, O. (1981). Are we all less risky and more skillful than our fellow drivers? *Acta Psychologica, 47,* 143–148.

Swann, W. B., Jr. (1984). Quest for accuracy in person perception: A matter of pragmatics. *Psychological Review, 91,* 457–477.

Swann, W. B., Jr., Giuliano, T., & Wegner, D. M. (1982). Where leading questions can lead: The power of conjecture in social interaction. *Journal of Personality and Social Psychology, 42,* 1025–1035.

Taylor, S. E., & Brown, J. D. (1988). Illusion and well-being: A social psychological perspective on mental health. *Psychological Bulletin, 103,* 193–210.

Tetlock, P. (1985). Accountability: A social check on the fundamental attribution error. *Social Psychology Quarterly, 48,* 227–236.

Thompson, E., Chaiken, S., & Hazlewood, P. (1993). Need for cognition and desire for control as moderators of extrinsic reward effects: A person x situation approach to the study of intrinsic motivation. *Journal of Personality and Social Psychology, 64,* 987–999.

Tiegen, K. (1986). Old truths or fresh insights? A study of students' evaluations of proverbs. *British Journal of Social Psychology, 25,* 43–49.

Tolman, E. C. (1932). *Purposive behavior in animals and men.* New York: Appleton-Century-Crofts.

Trope, Y. (1979). Uncertainty-reducing properties of achievement tasks. *Journal of Personality and Social Psychology, 37,* 1505–1518.

Trope, Y. (1980). Self-assessment and task performance. *Journal of Experimental Social Psychology, 18,* 201–215.

Trope, Y. (1986). Identification and inferential processes in dispositional attribution. *Psychological Review, 93,* 239–257.

Trope, Y., & Bassok, M. (1982). Confirmatory and diagnosing strategies in social information gathering. *Journal of Personality and Social Psychology, 43,* 22–34.

Trope, Y., & Bassok, M. (1983). Information gathering strategies in hypothesis-testing. *Journal of Experimental Social Psychology, 19,* 560–576.

Trope, Y., Bassok, M., & Alon, E. (1984). The questions lay interviewers ask. *Journal of Personality, 52,* 90–106.

Tulving, E. (1985). How many memory systems are there? *American Psychologist, 40,* 385–398.

Tversky, A., & Kahneman, D. (1980). Causal schemata in judgments under uncertainty. In M. Fishbein (Ed.), *Progress in social psychology* (pp. 49–72). Hillsdale, NJ: Lawrence Erlbaum Associates.

Wallach, A., & Wallach, L. (1983). *Psychology's sanction for selfishness: The error of egoism in theory and therapy.* San Francisco: Freeman.

Wason, P. C. (1966). Reasoning. In B. M. Foss (Ed.), *New horizons in psychology* (pp. 135–151). Harmondsworth, Middlesex, England: Penguin.

Wason, P. C., & Johnson-Laird, P. N. (1972). *Psychology of reasoning: Structure and content.* London: Batsford.

Webster, D. M. (1993). Motivated augmentation and reduction of the overattribution bias. *Journal of Personality and Social Psychology, 65,* 261–271.

Wegner, D. M., & Vallacher, R. R. (1981). Common-sense psychology. In J. P. Forgas (Ed.), *Social cognition: Perspectives on everyday understanding* (pp. 224–246). London: Academic.

Weiner, B. (1985). Spontaneous causal thinking. *Psychological Bulletin, 97,* 74–84.

Weiner, B. (1986). *An attributional theory of motivation and emotion.* New York: Springer Verlag.

Wellman, H. M., & Gelman, S. A. (1992). Cognitive development: Foundational theories of core domains. *Annual Review of Psychology, 43,* 337–375.

Wells, G. L., & Harvey, J. H. (1977). Do people use consensus information in making causal attributions? *Journal of Personality and Social Psychology, 35,* 270–293.

White, P. (1984). A model of the layperson as pragmatist. *Personality and Social Psychology Bulletin, 10,* 333–348.

Wilkes, K. V. (1993). The relationship between scientific psychology and common sense psychology. In S. M. Christensen & D. R. Turner (Eds.), *Folk psychology and the philosophy of mind* (pp. 167–187). Hillsdale, NJ: Lawrence Erlbaum Associates.

Author Index

Subject Index